Young Children at Home and in School

212 Educational Activities for Their Parents, Teachers, and Caregivers

Philip S. Morse

State University of New York College at Fredonia
Fredonia, New York

Lillian B. Brand

Hamburg Central Schools
Hamburg, New York

Allyn and Bacon

Boston   London   Toronto   Sydney   Tokyo   Singapore

Illustrations by: Charlotte Reimann Morse

Library of Congress Cataloging-in-Publication Data

Morse, Philip S.
    Young children at home and in school : 212 educational activities
  for their parents, teachers, and caregivers / Philip S. Morse,
  Lillian B. Brand.
      p.   cm.
    Includes bibliographical references and index.
    ISBN 0–205–15419–0 (cloth). — ISBN 0–205–15420–4 (paper)
    1. Educational games.   2. Creative activities and seat work.
  I. Brand, Lillian B.   II. Title.
LB1137.M68   1995
371.3'97--dc20   94–48395
                                                                  CIP

Printed in the United States of America
10   9   8   7   6   5   4   3   2   1   99   98   97   96   95

To our respective families,
especially Stephen and Julie Morse
and the Brand children and grandchildren

CONTENTS

CHAPTER THREE   Listening and Hearing   41

CHAPTER FOUR   Language   53

Assuming Responsibility   169

PREFACE

This is a book for parents and teachers of young children. It offers more than 200 activities in seven key areas: body movement, listening and hearing, language, looking and seeing, mathematics, science, and social and emotional development. These are more fully described in Chapter 1. All the activities are easy, enjoyable and educationally sound. They delight children and at the same time stimulate them in many areas of normal, healthy growth, including intellectual, emotional, physical, and social development.

The activities can be used up to and beyond the time when a child first begins formal schooling. Each activity is simple and practical. Almost all are without cost to the parent or teacher. Nearly all can be done in the child's home, school, or immediate neighborhood.

Explanatory material in each chapter helps the reader understand the reasons behind the activities. However, parents and teachers do not have to read this material in order to engage in the activities.

Each activity has been carefully chosen for developmental appropriateness and new and old concepts are constantly reinforced. Many of the activities are cross-referenced. Each activity lists at the end those other activities that relate to it. The child's understanding is enriched as he or she compares and contrasts related activities.

The activities are appropriate for anyone who works with or is responsible for young children—day care center practitioners, nursery school staff, prekindergarten, kindergarten, first-grade teachers, and, of course, parents. Other caregivers of young children also will find this book pertinent and valuable for their needs.

We encourage those who use this book to approach these activities in a spirit of playfulness and enthusiasm. Although many activities "teach" certain ideas important to a young child's development, the nature of learning in young children invites a flexible, nonstructured, and nondidactic approach. Try to follow the natural rhythm and tempo of the child and do the activities as he or she seems ready and receptive. Do not get discouraged if the child will not always "cooperate" with your well-laid plans.

Part of the wonder and mysteriousness of children's learning is its unpredictability. Have faith that the activities you present to your child, or to the children for whom you are responsible, will come alive either at the moment of presentation or at some future date. No effort is wasted and repetition is desirable as long as the child wants to participate in the activity.

ACKNOWLEDGMENTS

We are greatly indebted to many friends, colleagues, relatives, parents of preschool children, and others who have suggested activities for the book. We discovered that it was impossible to track down the sources of all the ideas. Like classic folklore, the best of a good idea often lingers on, with the author lost to antiquity. Many of the ideas are our own, and we have given credit to others when we were certain of the source. Our thanks to the anonymous originators of some of the ideas.

It is difficult to thank adequately all the people who have encouraged us, offered suggestions, and read various drafts of this book. We would particularly like to thank the following people who provided valuable critiques during various stages of completion: William Schall, Margaret Sawkins, Susan Theroux, Daniel Wheeler, Paula Roden, Richard Goldman, Betty Lynch, Arthur Robinson, Colleen McDonnell, Gail Kaney, and the New York State Pre-Kindergarten staff in Hamburg, New York. Also, our gratitude to Mary Iatridis, Patton Tabors, Steve Kane, Nancy Lauter-Klatell, Jone Sloman, Mira Berkley, and Mieko Kamii for their careful reading of and insightful suggestions for various chapters.

In particular, we would like to thank Sheila Jelly who wrote most of the science chapter. Her unselfish and generous contribution to the book not only defined a critical area in early childhood education but also reinforced important philosophical concepts and ideas in the education and experience of young children.

Our gratitude to Joan Costley for the generous giving of her time and valuable support, help, and writing contributions to Chapter 1.

Thanks also to Catherine Snow, Courtney Cazden, Jeanne Chall, Kurt Fischer, Lowry Hemphill, Allyssa McCabe, Victoria Purcell-Gates, David Dickinson, Edith Allison, and Barbara Kerner for their help and counsel.

And, particular appreciation goes to Ross and Frona Vicksell for their overall material generosity and moral support while *Young Children at Home and in School* was being prepared.

We would especially like to thank Margaret B. Morse for her time-consuming, thorough, patient, infallible, and expert scrutiny of the logic of sentence structure, usage, spelling, and general organization of the text. Her determination and dedication have been a big factor in helping make this book a reality.

We are ever grateful to our respective families for their patience and understanding.

We also wish to thank Marilyn Rash of Ocean Publication Services for her sure-handed, professional guidance as our editor.

Finally, we would like to thank the children and their parents with whom we have worked. From their positive responses to many of the ideas contained in these pages, they inspired us to keep going. Without their warmth, responsibility, and interest, it would have been difficult for us to sustain the effort required to complete this book.

ABOUT THE AUTHORS

Philip S. Morse is a professor in the Education Department at the State University of New York College at Fredonia. He has presented at numerous national, state, and local conferences, consulted in many school districts, and has written widely on the teaching of writing, thinking, and early childhood education. Dr. Morse has held appointments as a visiting scholar at the Graduate School of Education at the University of California at Berkeley and Harvard University. He is presently studying the communication skills teachers use in their classrooms and how such techniques can enhance learning. As a trained mediator, Dr. Morse is also investigating the subject of conflict resolution and its application to learning environments—nursery school through twelfth grade—and how peer mediation can support a positive classroom climate.

Lillian B. Brand is the director of early childhood education for the Hamburg Central School District in Hamburg, New York, and is currently serving as principal of the Charlotte Avenue Elementary School. She is also co-director of CEC Consultants—a network of professional educators providing resources to early childhood programs. She is currently on the board of directors of the New York State Pre-Kindergarten Administrators' Association. Mrs. Brand is past president of the Early Childhood Education Council of Western New York and has served as an early childhood consultant for the New York State Education Department, as well as for public schools and private organizations. The author of several articles on parent education, Mrs. Brand has appeared before many parent and teacher groups speaking on early childhood.

Young Children
at Home and in School

CHAPTER ONE

Principles, Programs, and Resources

The significant adults in young children's lives are their first teachers. Many of the things children learn before entering formal schooling stay with them for the rest of their lives. That is why parents, teachers, relatives, and others can be such a positive influence on the lives of young children. Although much learning takes place spontaneously as children interact with their environment, adults can help sharpen and stimulate natural learning. Also, adults can help create moments and events that will heighten children's love of learning.

The ideas on the following pages tie in with children's natural curiosity and joy of discovery. One of the nicest things about their fascination with the world is the confident, optimistic feeling children can get when they are able to explore their surroundings freely.

As adults, we often view playfulness with a vague sense of apology and even embarrassment, as if we are not quite deserving of its joys. Yet, the playfulness of children is essential to the healthy mental functioning of adults and children alike.

Playfulness has many faces. For example, the playfulness of scientists, like the playfulness of children, is intense, allowing both to explore and try out a wide range of ideas with no fear of being wrong (Duckworth et al., 1990, p. 8). Learning is a messy and unpredictable process and children, especially young ones, need to explore, examine, and observe freely as a way of making sense of the world around them.

Playfulness is vital to the interaction between adult and child—simply having fun, enjoying the experience of being together, and sharing the environment in a mutual journey of discovery. In an early childhood setting, the dialogue between student and teacher, and student and student, is what David Hawkins, a well-known science education expert, describes as the *I-Thou-It* relationship, which consists of the teacher, student, and the external world (Hawkins, 1974, p. 48). With the presence of materials and other stimuli for learning in a fully functioning classroom, the student not only can interact with and "mess about," or play with these resources, but also can communicate and discuss with the teacher and his or her peers the "Its" that engross him or her.

The spirit of playfulness also can be defined as active, curious wonderment:

A child's world is fresh and new and beautiful, full of wonder and excitement. It is our misfortune that for most of us that clear-eyed vision, that true instinct for what is beautiful and awe-inspiring, is dimmed and even lost before we reach adulthood. If I had influence with the good fairy who is supposed to preside over the christening of all children, I should ask that her gift to each child in the world be a sense of wonder so indestructible that it would last throughout life, as an unfailing antidote against the boredom and disenchantments of later years, the sterile preoccupation with things that are artificial, the alienation from the sources of our strength.

If a child is to keep alive his inborn sense of wonder without any such gift from the fairies, he needs the companionship of at least one adult who can share it, rediscovering with him the joy, excitement and mystery of the world we live in (Carson, 1987, pp. 42–43).

PRINCIPLES OF EARLY CHILDHOOD PROGRAMS

A frequent concern for both parent and teacher centers around the kinds of environments that will most stimulate and nurture the playfulness so conducive to young children's active, healthy development. The following are important ingredients of an effective early childhood program either at home or at school:

1. *A child is an active, crucial agent in his or her learning process.* Learning results from the self-initiated, individual interaction with the world children inhabit. In "messing about" with their environment, children are driven by a love of learning and by a fine curiosity to make sense and order of the puzzlement of our world (Duckworth et al., 1990, p. 3). In encouraging children's learning, we want to nurture delight in the unexpected and use curiosity as a natural learning tool.

Individual children interact capably with almost any element in their environment and learn something from it. Such elements include toys, role-playing and play, manipulative materials, teachers, and peers. People's reactions to children and their activities help them gain a realistic perspective and understanding not only in their subsequent interactions with other people but also in the comprehension of the properties and uses of things in the environment. Conducive to the above is a multi-faceted, flexible classroom setting where many activities happen simultaneously. Children can talk and move freely about in such an environment, interacting with their peers, teachers, and other adults. Such settings also have the room's contents accessible to all children.

2. *Learning is a natural, lifelong process.* Learning is an integrated, informal, but purposeful evolution of social and intellectual skills. Early childhood activities at home or at school do not lend themselves to neat subdivisions of the disciplines of knowledge. Subject matter areas intimately relate to each other and cannot be readily divorced from one another.

3. *Young children learn from older children when they share activities.* Multi-aged grouping leads to a corresponding variety of ability and talent which in turn offers greater possibilities for seeing oneself in various perspectives. Children's self-image can grow if they can observe freely and reflect on others' strengths and weaknesses. Flexible peer-interactions provide role models in the persons of older children. Therefore, younger children often learn more quickly what people expect of them.

4. *There is a de-emphasis on competition among peers in activities shared by older and younger children.* In a varied classroom or family environment children cannot compete so readily when each engages in a different task. Also, encouraging cooperation among children in a positive, interdependent classroom community or family enhances the social skills so important for success in later life.

5. *Freedom from fear of failure.* Fear of failure often happens less in an environment where children learn they can benefit from mistakes and not have to hide from their errors to avoid ridicule. Children do not fail if they are able to adjust to errors, rather than having these totaled up against them by teachers or peers. The lack of fear of failure also supports and encourages children to explore new ideas.

6. *Adults as facilitators.* Although children learn much as autonomous agents in such a climate, the teacher or parent can best determine whether the environment will suppress or encourage children's developing sense of their relationship to the latter. For example, a good early childhood education teacher eases children into situations where learning can happen and supports their curiosities and discoveries rather than always presenting the answers. Through the communication skills of open-ended questions, active listening, and nonverbal behavior, such as eye contact and attentive body language, a teacher or parent offers opportunities and an environment from which children can formulate their own questions and derive their own satisfactory answers. Teachers and parents become sensitive listeners and responders, helping children in their quest for understanding.

As children become engrossed in the world around them, the guiding adult encourages them to plumb the depths by acting as a facilitator, resource person, helping agent, and organizer of the environment that reflects children's needs and capabilities.

7. *Community, and especially parent support constitute an important element in an effective early childhood program.* Parents can participate in a program in numerous ways, including offering skills and experience in the classroom, helping teachers with housekeeping, creating needed materials, and serving in the library or in other areas. Also, training or retraining anyone involved in a program is a vital component in promoting and maintaining its vitality and continuity.

In conclusion, successful early childhood education should be a matter of spontaneity, surprise, and delight in the unexpected—a series of question marks rather than the provision of a set of periods. It is important to look at the learning children do as a whole event—a sum total of all the bits and pieces of stimuli, remembrances, and interactions with family members, classmates, and the teacher.

When one offers real, genuine, significant learning, one speaks of learning that comes from discovery, from finding structure and order in the searchings and explorations of an individual. Carl Rogers (1994) describes the essential components of what he labels as significant or experiential learning:

> One element is the quality of *personal involvement:* The whole person, both in feeling and in cognitive aspects, is part of the learning event. *Self-initiated* involvement is

another element. Even when the impetus or stimulus comes from the outside, the sense of discovery, of reaching out, of grasping and comprehending comes from within. Another element is *pervasiveness*. It makes a difference in the behavior, the attitudes, perhaps even the personality of the learner. Yet another element relates to the learner's *evaluation* of the event. She knows whether it is meeting her need, whether it leads toward what she wants to know, whether it illuminates her dark area of ignorance. The locus of evaluation, we might say, resides definitely in the learner. *Its essence is meaning.* When such learning takes place, the element of meaning to the learner is built into the whole experience (p. 36).

Finally, Carson (1987) asks what value there is in preserving and strengthening the sense of awe and wonder. She asks whether the exploration of the natural world is just a pleasant way of occupying young children's time and attention or whether there is something deeper. Her answer:

I am sure there is something much deeper, something lasting and significant. Those who dwell, as scientists or laymen, among the beauties and mysteries of the earth are never alone or weary of life. Whatever the vexations or concerns of their personal lives, their thoughts can find paths that lead to inner contentment and to renewed excitement in living. Those who contemplate the beauty of the earth find reserves of strength that will endure as long as life lasts. There is symbolic as well as actual beauty in the migration of the birds, the ebb and flow of the tides, the folded bud ready for the spring. There is something infinitely healing in the repeated refrains of nature—the assurance that dawn comes after night, and spring after the winter (pp. 88–89).

THE HOME–SCHOOL CONNECTION

To apply the philosophy of early childhood activities, it is immediately important to examine the relationship of parent to early childhood practitioner or, more specifically, to look in detail at how the teacher and parent can work together in exchanging materials, ideas, and resources for the benefit of the child.

One of the key changes in the lives of young children in our country during the past twenty years has taken place because of the major changes in patterns of family life. As of 1990, more than half of the young children in the United States had mothers in the workforce (U.S. Census Bureau, 1990). Also, it is increasingly likely that a child will spend at least a portion of his or her childhood in a single-parent family—either with a mother or a father—or in blended families created by divorce and remarriage. Grandparents or other family members may also live with the family. One of the consequences of these changes is that young children spend a substantial portion of their time in the care of adults other than their parents—in preschool programs such as pre-kindergarten, nursery school, child care centers, Head Start programs and family child care homes. Today's families are learning how to develop a new kind of relationship with early care and education practitioners. Teachers of young children have been characterized as "the new extended family" (Galinsky, 1977) for the children and their parents.

For that reason, there are a number of ways that some of the activities in this book, as well as the idea of shared play, can validate a child's family experience, involve family members in the child's daily life, and address the idea of the increasingly diverse family constellations. For example, both teachers and parents can begin defining more clearly the meaning of family diversity by beginning to talk with children about "all of the people in your or our family—the ones who live in this house and the ones who don't."

The activities in this book are designed to be flexible and require virtually no specialized materials. Teachers and parents will find that the activities can be used in a variety of situations—with individual children, with small groups of children, or with larger groups. The developmental range the activities cover is also one that lends itself well to mixed age groups of young children. The same activity may be easy for one child and more of a challenge for another. The book is equally adaptable for use by parents at home with their children and for teachers at school. Teachers can play a supportive role in helping parents understand the book's benefits and begin to feel comfortable using the activities.

Although parents often are told that they are their child's "first teacher," what exactly does that mean? The intention of this phrase is to reassure parents of their importance in their child's learning experiences; however, many parents, especially those whose first language is not English or who have not had much formal education, may be intimidated by this responsibility. They may feel that they are being asked to take on a task beyond their skills, or that they are being asked to "drill" their child or teach in the formal ways they remember from their own early school experiences. Even without these barriers, many parents are not familiar with the kind of open-ended, developmental approach to exploratory learning that these activities represent. It will be mutually beneficial for parents and teachers to share and enjoy the activities presented in this book.

The fact that teachers use the activities in this book may help both parents and children to make the transition to enjoying them together at home. Young children are very willing to share songs, games, words, and activities they have enjoyed with people they care about. Discovering that the parent is already aware of the activities reinforces children's sense of continuity and community among the adults in their lives. Knowing that a child has already tried some of the activities takes some of the pressure off for the parent to be the expert. It allows parents and children to enjoy the activity together and at times lets a child be the expert.

There are a number of approaches teachers might use to acquaint parents with activities in this book and their value to children. One of the most enjoyable might be to invite parents to come, with their children, to a potluck supper, a morning coffee, or afternoon tea at which the teacher can share with the parents what their children are doing during the day. Many parents appreciate the opportunity to spend time at their children's program, center, or family child care home before they begin their day. The availability of coffee and/or juice and snacks creates a hospitable atmosphere. This can be a relaxed way for parents to become more at ease with the teacher and with one another, and it builds the trust necessary for success.

At some point during the time everyone is together, the teacher can offer to do a demonstration of some of the activities with the children as both information and entertainment for the children and the parents alike. Once they have seen the demonstration of some of the activities, invite parents to join in. In all probability not all of them will feel comfortable immediately, although perhaps they will! The teacher and parents can try asking children which activity they enjoy, and then have them demonstrate the activity. At this point, the teacher and parents can easily move around the room to provide encouragement and additional information. After the demonstration, it becomes less intimidating to hear about the learning and the developmental value of these activities—all have experienced the fun first.

The activities should be presented as a game or fun activity or in response to a child wanting to initiate an activity. In this context, parents are reassured that if they and their child are enjoying the activity, there are many benefits that are generated naturally. This also holds true for the school setting. For example, a child learns that the parent and the teacher value the time spent with him or her. Also, the joint play makes the child feel that her or his interests and activities are important. In addition, when the parent or teacher is able to engage in the activity without emphasizing what the child is doing right or wrong, the child develops a sense of confidence in exploration and play.

One of the realities of contemporary family life is its often hectic quality. To help parents avoid the feeling that doing these activities with their child is "one more thing they have to do," it can be helpful to emphasize that brief play sessions, including the ones spontaneously initiated by the child, are equally valuable and more likely to happen than a carefully planned "play hour." Teachers can suggest that there are numerous times during a day when one of these activities can be combined with other family routines. In fact, they may reduce some of the stress both parents and children encounter in getting through a typical day or week. Some examples of times to use an activity at home are:

• During bath or washing up time
• While doing laundry
• At the supermarket while the child rides in the carry seat of the grocery cart
• During a walk in the neighborhood to do an errand
• While preparing dinner or after dinner while washing dishes
• As a fun time before bedtime
• On the way home together from the early childhood program (a very enjoyable way to pass the time, especially on public transportation)

Over time and with familiarity, the child may develop variations of his or her own. It is helpful to let the parent know that this is an indication of the child's creativity and curiosity rather than a mistake and is something to be praised and encouraged. This also makes the child feel like a partner in the playtime.

Teachers, in addition to inviting parents in for a group meeting, may find it useful to share written versions of the activities through a "news-sheet" that goes home with each child.

In many families men are not used to seeing themselves as part of their child's play activities. Not only fathers, but also grandfathers, uncles, and important family friends need a great deal of encouragement to feel at home in a world they see as belonging to women. The good news is that many of them are only too delighted to be included when they feel that their presence is truly seen as valued and valuable. Increased attention is being paid to the issue of how to involve men successfully in their child's learning experiences from the earliest year (Levine, Murphy, and Wilson, 1993).

Parents and teachers can participate in children's play by talking about the following:

- Games you used to play as a child.
- Songs and rhymes you remember from your childhood.
- What you used to do to have fun when you were a child.
- How you learned things when you were a child.

These suggestions apply to any community or country, for play is a worldwide phenomenon. Children and adults may discover that even though words or language may be different, many songs and play activities are very much alike around the world.

In the school setting when a family member or friend comes to the group to share some experiences with the children, think about ways to make a record of what they bring and do. Taking snapshots for display on a bulletin board, making audio- or videotapes of the adults' visits, and creating a notebook can help create memories for all of the children. If the theme of play is interwoven with other activities throughout the year, the teacher will find a rich and unique collection of ideas, activities, and stories of childhood that can be shared with the children and the parents.

COMMUNICATING WITH THE CHILD

Two areas that are vital to children's maturing relationship with the world are their ability to communicate with themselves and those around them, and their capacity to get along with others. Effective parenting and teaching depend on certain universal principles of effective communication, particularly those that pertain to children (Morse, 1994).

Children are honest. Trustworthy feedback, which is natural to good communication, works well with children because they can sense a sincere response. They are still able to react with the genuineness of a person who has not yet developed the roles, affectations, and defenses of adults. Because so much is still new and different for them, they are open to being influenced by what people say to them, especially when those with whom they are interacting are the significant adults in their lives.

The potential for adults being a positive influence in the lives of children is enormous, especially when we examine the ways adults can introduce and reinforce children's new understandings. We reach others by verbal and nonverbal communication. Whether we react negatively to a temper tantrum or find delight in "cuteness," the way we respond to children affects their self-esteem, their confidence, their ability to risk, and their ability to deal with problems and crises in their lives.

All people have certain identifiable needs unique to them. Some needs are easier to identify and deal with than others. Because young children are just beginning to grasp the subtleties and power of words, much of what they say and do is done through the overt expression and acting out of feelings. Consequently, adults must sometimes guess at what children really want. For example, if a daughter consistently pushes or hits other children, it is often productive to try to determine what might be bothering her rather than punishing her or telling her to stop doing that. A parent's ability to listen to another, to empathize with her position, to try to understand what makes her do or say what she does is one of the keys to effective communication.

Carl Rogers, the internationally known psychologist, based his philosophy and principles of communication on three elements: a deeply sensitive nonjudgmental understanding of the individual, caring, and realness. These are as pertinent for three-year-olds as they are for people in their eighties. According to

Rogers (1994), the ability of parents, teachers, coaches, physicians, psychotherapists, psychologists, social workers, clergy, and other helping agents to practice these skills corresponds with their effectiveness as communicators. Rogers defines helping agents as those individuals who can support and help others by being able to listen effectively, offer encouragement, and otherwise be sensitive to another person's feelings and needs.

The universality of Rogers's theories lies in his belief that if a person truly tries to understand another and genuinely respects that person's feelings and what he or she has to say, this respect is what effects growth and change. The concept of empathy involves trying to perceive how another person might be feeling or what one seems to be going through, getting thoroughly and completely into the other's frame of reference.

Caring or positive regard is equally important to good communication. It means a nonjudgmental attitude toward the other person with neither an expression of approval or disapproval. It is a genuine acceptance of another with all the understanding that one can muster. It is a trusting of a person's inner resources and potential for positive change. Positive regard is a demonstration that one person accepts another as he or she is without qualification or doubt about the other's abilities or capacities for growth.

Finally, genuineness or realness involves an honest sharing of how the person is understanding the other and what he or she is feeling as one tries to grasp that person's world. Rogers states that it is sobering to observe how seldom people really listen to what others say. But without real attention there can be no true understanding and hence no real communication. Apparently it is difficult for most people to listen carefully to another person because they are too intent on what they will say when the other person stops speaking. Because listening behavior is so important, most definitions of helping relationships stress the importance of one person listening to another with real understanding (Corsini, 1984, p. 164).

Using Rogers's ideas of empathic understanding, caringness, and genuineness, Allen Ivey (1992), a nationally known counseling psychologist, and his associates have developed a model that is equally applicable to good parenting and teaching. The following sections define the essential elements of good communication skills pertinent to children.

Basic Attending Behavior

1. *Eye contact*—look at the child from time to time but do not stare. Making "gentle" eye contact reassures her or him that you are paying attention or "attending" to what she or he is saying.
2. *Attentive body language*—be natural and assume a comfortable body posture. Leaning forward slightly, together with a relaxed, easy posture most often communicates your being attentive and interested in the child.
3. *Natural use of voice*—speak in a normal, warm, friendly, accepting tone of voice.

Gentle Encouragement

According to Thomas Gordon (1974), another well-known psychologist, there are a number of gentle responses or minimal encouragements that will prompt the child to continue talking:

1. *Silence*—saying nothing at all, but being attentive and interested in what the child is saying, is an effective way of conveying genuine acceptance and encouragement.
2. *Acknowledgment responses*—often referred to as "empathic grunting," acknowledgment responses use cues like, "I see," or "Uh-huh" and often include head nods and a variety of other nonverbal body postures or gestures that let the child know you are listening.
3. *Door openers*—these consist of a few words or short sentences that are in response to something the child said and encourage him or her to continue. Examples include, "Tell me more," "Give me an example," "That's something I'd like to hear more about," or "How did you feel about that?" It also could be one or two key words from the child's past statements.

Active or Reflective Listening

Active listening is a process of sending back to the speaker what you as a listener think the speaker meant—both in terms of content and feelings. For example, suppose a child is excluded from playing a game with other children and says, "They won't let me play with them." If the parent or teacher is practicing active listening, he or she might respond, "That must be a little upsetting to you that they won't let you play." You are checking in with the message sender to see whether you heard his or her message accurately. To do this you need to send feedback and mirror what you *think* the child is saying, both verbally and nonverbally. The listener does not repeat the child's exact word-for-word utterances but rather reflects back on what the listener believes the essence of the message to be.

In short, active listening is a way for the listener to indicate to the speaker that the message content and the speaker's feelings were understood. From the child's reaction, the listener can determine whether he or she is on the right track in determining what the child is really trying to say. The receiver continues to send out accurate namings of feelings and what he or she thinks the content of the child's message is until the child seems satisfied that this is indeed what she or he is trying to say.

There are a number of different ways a person can begin an active listening response. The following sentence stems or leads are a few examples:

"Kind of feeling . . ."
"As I hear it, you . . ."
"Listening to you it seems as if . . ."
"If I'm hearing you right . . ."
"I think that you're feeling . . ."
"You feel, perhaps . . ."
"I'm picking up that you . . ."
"So, as you see it . . ."
"I wonder if you're saying . . ."
"What I hear you saying is that . . ."
"You feel . . ."
"As I get it, you're saying . . ."
"So you feel . . ."
"So let me see if I have this right . . ."
"It seems to you . . ."

A simpler form of active listening is merely paraphrasing back what the child said without trying to determine what the feelings or thoughts are behind the message. For example, a six-year-old might say, "I'm wondering about the play we're having—do my parents have to come?" If you were merely reflecting back or paraphrasing what the child is saying, you might respond with something like, "You're not sure about whether your parents are supposed to come?" If you were trying to practice active listening, you would try to determine what is behind the child's question. It might be, "You're worried that both your father and mother can't or won't come?" It is taking a response or a question one step further and trying to determine what is on the child's mind that would make her or him say or ask the question. To do that, you test the waters by trying out various responses to see if that is what the child is thinking and/or feeling.

In summary, when parents or teachers are practicing active listening, their responses accomplish two things: (1) They show the child that the adult is listening, and (2) they encourage the child to continue—either confirming or correcting the listener's attempt at clarification.

Many who begin practicing active listening initially worry about what they are going to say and whether their response is "correct." It is worth noting that for any given message there are dozens of different ways a good listener can respond. It is best not to fret about the perfect response, but rather to respond naturally to whatever the child has said. A listener need only stay with what a child seems to be saying and "give back" to the child what the listener thinks he or she is trying to express.

Finally, the following questions from Faraday and Harris (1994) can help one listen actively:

- Am I able, and do I care enough, to give the child my full attention?
- Do I really prefer talking to listening?
- Am I thinking about the effect I am having on the child?
- What sort of signs and clues am I giving physically and verbally?
- Do I hear what I expect, or want to hear?
- Do I listen for hidden messages, both what is said and how it is said?
- Am I distinguishing between what the child says is the problem and what is the real problem?

Reflection of Feelings

Many children's responses come from feelings that reflect or relate to something that happened or might happen in their lives. Parents and teachers can help children sort out facts from emotions. Helping identify emotions is, once again, a way of showing children that you care, and that you are listening. The reflection of feelings involves a reflection of children's emotional states.

The following are some guidelines for practicing effective reflection of feelings (Ivey, Gluckstern, and Ivey, 1992):

- Use the child's name from time to time and/or use the pronoun "you."
- The feelings must be labeled as specifically and vividly as possible. Give special attention to mixed or ambivalent feelings.
- Use sentence fragments or stems such as, "You seem to feel . . ." "Sounds as if you feel . . ." "John (or any name), I sense you're _____" (add the labeled emotion).
- The context may be paraphrased for additional clarification: "You seem to feel . . . when you . . ."
- Reflection of feelings is most often useful if immediate here-and-now feelings are labeled and worked through.

The following excerpt is an example of a teacher concentrating on a child's emotional content:

CHILD: "I'm going to spend the whole summer with my grand-
        parents!"
TEACHER: "You seem to feel pretty excited about staying with
        them for the summer."
CHILD: "Yeah, I sort of am, but I'm wondering whether there
        will be anyone my age down there."
TEACHER: "You're happy about going, but you might also be
        feeling a little anxious about not having anyone to talk
        to."
CHILD: "I don't want to be by myself all summer."
TEACHER: "Sounds as if you will feel lonely if no one is around."

Open Invitation to Talk

Inviting a child to discuss topics of interest to him is best achieved by a response in the form of a question. There are two kinds—open and closed. Closed questions often are factual in nature, frequently begin with "is" or "are," and can usually be answered by a simple "yes" or "no."

Open questions often begin with "what," "how," "could," or "would." Questions beginning with "what" lead a child to talk about the details of a situation ("What happened when you saw your cat was frightened by a truck?"). "How" questions most often help a child to talk about process, sequence, and emotions ("How did you feel when you heard about that?"). Questions that begin with "could" or "would" tend to provide the maximum amount of room for a response ("Could you tell me more about your visit?"). For example, in going back to the dialogue under active listening in this chapter, where the child was excluded from a game by playmates, the listener in that case could ask a follow-up question, "Would you like to ask them anything?" in attempting to help resolve the matter in as open and flexible a way as possible.

It should be noted that closed-ended questions tend to put people on the defensive ("Why is she asking me that?"). Similarly, questions that begin with "why" can make children feel interrogated. For example, if you ask a child who is drawing a picture, "Why didn't you include the color of your car?", it may be impossible to answer and also could make the student feel that she or he has done something wrong in some vague, ill-defined way.

Finding the Positive

Rogers's emphasis on positive regard can be translated into what Ivey calls "The Positive Asset Search" (Ivey et al., 1992). We all need to be recognized and receive attention of some sort. Often, people react negatively when they aren't noticed, affirmed, acknowledged, or validated in some way at least once in a while. Children are no exception. A simple touch or a smile will sometimes communicate as much or more than any words can.

To be distinguished from generic praise that is often empty, general, or implies a judgmental stance ("You're a good girl"), finding the positive or the positive asset search is the sincere identification of something specifically positive that a child has done, a well-intentioned effort at something, or simply noticing that the child exists. For example, you can comment on a new dress, the fact that a child looks happy, or that you like her or his choice of words in describing something. The emphasis on strength and not weakness is what helps children grow and also strengthens and increases self-esteem.

Often, you will be using these communication skills as a way of resolving conflicts or trying to solve a problem that the child has or one that comes up when interacting with peers. In those cases, the parent or teacher is in effect a mediator and helps the child or children deal with the issues at hand. Not only is the adult a model for resolving conflict but he or she can provide words, a process, and rationality to the event. For example, let's assume that two four-year-olds get into a tug of war over a toy truck. The following is a sample dialogue between the adult and the two children in conflict:

ADULT: "Stephen, would you like to talk to Jason about the truck?"

STEPHEN: "It's my truck. I want it back."

ADULT: "I hear Stephen saying that he wants his truck back. How do you feel about that Jason?"

JASON: "I had it first."

ADULT: "Jason, you're saying you had it first. Does anyone have any ideas for what we can do?"

JASON: "He can play with it after I'm done."

ADULT: "How does that sound to you, Stephen?"

STEPHEN: "I want it now."

ADULT: "It seems that both of you want the truck immediately. What can we do so that both of you can play with the truck right now?"

JASON: "Stephen can have it after I push it over to the sink."

ADULT: "Stephen, how do you like that idea?" (*Stephen nods and looks happy.*)

ADULT: "Terrific! It looks as if the two of you have found a solution to the problem."

The adult is using active listening, open-ended questioning, and positive reinforcement in an attempt to resolve the problem and at the same time is subtly showing how cooperation, negotiation, and agreement can effect a solution. Children are naturally egocentric, and, in this case, the adult can show how conflicts can be resolved by discussion and how the parties can ultimately arrive at a fair and equitable consensus if both are willing to cooperate.

Being willing to negotiate with children also shows an implicit respect and trust for the feelings of the child and faith that children can learn to become problem solvers for themselves. Rather than punish children, you create a setting where they can engage in the process of negotiation, give and take, and learn to work out their difficulties with their own resources. With the high rate of imprisonment and recidivism today, society has already demonstrated how the legal system is often ineffective in dealing with asocial behavior, especially if the person has not internalized the set of standards that society demands. Nonjudgmentally dealing with conflicts and the violation of limits, and using a no-lose problem-solving approach gives children confidence and self-esteem—they are worthy of respect, are able to solve problems themselves, and can expect a fair and just settlement.

In an adult-centered environment where rules are paramount and punishment is the way conflicts are usually resolved, children learn to behave differently when adults watch, depend on adults for solutions, rely on external controls, repress and inhibit feelings, conform to the group, evade punishment, and blame each other. In a child-centered approach, kids learn to respect themselves and others, accept responsibility, think for themselves, express feelings, empathize with others, and solve problems (Reynolds, 1990).

OVERVIEW OF BOOK

As mentioned in the preface, this book deals with the following seven key areas in a child's overall physical, intellectual, social, and emotional development:

1. *Body movement,* including body awareness and the coordination of large and small muscles of the body.

2. *Auditory discrimination,* or listening and hearing, is vital to a young child's developing sense of the world of sounds and their significance to his or her immediate world. That

chapter includes sections on differentiating sounds and re-membering sounds.

3. *Language skills* are closely connected with both listening and seeing. The chapter on language includes sections on language concepts, vocabulary, and logical thinking—three sub-categories vital to language development.

4. *Visual discrimination,* or looking and seeing, is equally impor-tant. Recognizing colors, identifying shapes, telling left from right, and learning letters are the four areas in that chapter.

5. The *mathematics* chapter deals with mathematical processes, counting, time concepts, and recognizing numbers.

6. *Science* reinforces mathematical concepts but also stimulates language and visual and auditory discrimination. Many sci-ence activities deal with observation of the natural world, sorting, classifying, and making logical conclusions about the environment. Both science and mathematics are key areas in understanding the world in which we live.

7. The *social–emotional* chapter covers a number of important areas including the reinforcement of one's self-concept, rela-tionships with others, and assuming responsibility. Also included in this chapter are conflict resolution strategies, discussion of cultural diversity issues, and communication skills.

As much as possible, activities are presented sequentially in individual chapters according to age and maturity level. However, children (and even adults) often do not learn in an orderly fashion so skip around freely and do not worry if you do not seem to be presenting activities in a controlled or logical way. In fact, children may become disheartened if they are forced to conform to a par-ticular sequence of learning activities.

Try to relate the activities to each other as much as possible. Many are cross-referenced, but, on your own, you may find one ac-tivity leading quite naturally and unexpectedly into another. Each activity has a description of what is being attempted, but, often, with a particular activity, many other skills are reinforced at the same time. Many activities list others that are related to it.

Parents and teachers need not worry about repeating any of these activities. Children will benefit from repetition and often take pleasure in it. Many activities introduce children to new ideas that need to be repeated and reinforced many times in different contexts before they will be able to grasp them fully. Children gain complete understanding of new ideas only through experiences with the ideas in a variety of concrete, real-life situations.

Present these activities in a relaxed manner. It is best to let children seek out their readiness level naturally and spontaneously. Normal, healthy children have different physical and mental "timetables" for development. Pushing in the hope that this will speed up development is often fruitless and may unnecessarily frustrate a child or even set him or her back because of possible feelings of discouragement. The activities are not meant to accelerate development but to strengthen, solidify, and reinforce skills already emerging. Be willing to drop an activity temporarily if a child does not seem ready or interested. You may find that the idea may be perfectly suitable the following week or month. The child is the only person who can determine his or her own readiness.

More than anything, learning can and should be enjoyable. Childhood only happens once for a precious, few years. Make the most out of it for both you and the child.

REFERENCES

Carson, R. (1987). *The sense of wonder.* New York: HarperCollins.

Corsini, R. J. (1984). *Current psychotherapies.* Itasca, IL: F. E. Peacock Publishers, Inc.

Duckworth, E., Easley, J., Hawkins, D., Henriques, A. (1990). *Science education: A minds-on approach for the elementary years.* Hillsdale, NJ: Lawrence Erlbaum Associates, Publishers.

Faraday, S., and Harris, R. (1994). *Learning support: A staff development resource pack for those working with learners who have special needs.* London, England: Further Education Unit, Training Agency, National Bureau of Students with Disabilities.

Galinsky, E. (1977). *The new extended family: Day care that works.* Boston: Houghton Mifflin.

Gordon, Thomas (1974). *Teacher effectiveness training.* New York: Longman Publishers.

Hawkins, D. (1974). *The informed vision: Essays on learning and human nature.* New York: Agathon Press.

Ivey, A. E., Gluckstern, N. B., Ivey, M. B. (1992). *Basic attending skills* (3rd ed.). North Amherst, MA: Microtraining Associates.

Levine, J. A., Murphy, D. T., Wilson, C. (1993). *Getting men involved: Strategies for early childhood programs.* New York: Scholastic Inc.

Morse, Philip S. (1994). The writing teacher as helping agent: Communicating effectively in the conferencing process. *Journal of Classroom Interaction, 29*(1): 9–15.

Reynolds, E. (1990). *Guiding young children: A child-centered approach.* Mountain View, CA: Mayfield Publishing Company.

Rogers, C., Freiberg, H. J. (1994). *Freedom to learn* (3rd ed.). New York: Merrill.

U.S. Census Bureau. (1990). *Who's minding the kids? Child care arrangements 1986–1987* (Current Population Report, Series P-70, No. 20). Washington, DC: U.S. Government Printing Office.

CHAPTER TWO

Body Movement

Perceptual motor development is the ability to understand and interpret the world through physical movement. Being able to move with intelligence and purpose is a characteristic of nearly all human beings. Motor abilities begin developing even before birth, for the unborn infant is capable of considerable movement in the womb.

The newborn infant soon begins to learn about the physical qualities of the immediate environment. Muscle coordination evolves from the simplest activities such as reaching for a rattle or waving arms and legs in excitement. Gradually a child learns to control and direct movement in response to the information received through the senses. By the time a child is of school age, she or he has learned to sit up, creep, stand, walk, climb, jump, and perform more complicated tasks like pulling a wagon or even riding a bicycle.

As parents you will delight in watching your child's exciting, all-out efforts as he or she learns to roll over, sit, stand, and walk. You will offer constant encouragement, urging your child to "come to Mommy" or "bring it to Daddy." Your child will, of course, take great pleasure in your encouragement and thrive on it. Recent research supports the view that enjoyable early motor experiences influence the later development of cognitive and thinking skills. The developing child needs time and space to experiment, practice, and integrate emerging perceptual-motor skills. The following sections represent three areas that focus on the kinds of skills your child will need to develop perceptual-motor abilities: body awareness, coordinating large muscles, and coordinating small muscles.

BODY AWARENESS

The term *body awareness* is more than the visual image or outward appearance of the body. It is a strong awareness of the body and its parts as an integrated or functioning mass or whole. The awareness of one's body is constantly being modified and refined as one experiences and experiments with its potential and its limitations. Early awareness of body image seems to develop from the young child's "try-and-see" approach. One example of a young child's learning about body capacity is the realization that he cannot push his body through the rungs of a crib. He learns from imme-

diate experience that his head and shoulders will not fit through the rungs. Gradually, such information enables the baby to gain an awareness of what his body can and cannot do.

During infancy the awareness of total body is nonspecific. As the child grows and develops, she learns that her body has specific parts that have specific functions. For instance, she may move one leg and not the other, or swing her arms in opposite directions. The body and its parts begin to take on more and more individuality.

Freedom of movement is basic to a child's ability to develop a sense of his body in the space around him. He experiments continually with his body as it relates to his immediate environment. For example, a child will discover that his whole hand will not fit into the small round opening of a birdhouse. He will learn that one, or possibly two fingers is the limit of his body's ability to enter the hole meant for a bird.

Activities 1, 2, and 5 involve a basic awareness of parts of the body. Activity 3 combines the task of getting dressed with using certain body parts. Activity 4 coordinates an awareness of the body with the task of moving through an obstacle course, and Activity 6 relates the giving of oral directions to the identification and use of certain body parts.

Activity 1   "Touch Your Nose, Touch Your Toes"
Naming Parts of the Body

DIRECTIONS: Ask your child to touch a part of her body, using such directions as "Touch your head," "Touch your toes," "Touch your ear," "Touch your leg." Then let your child call out the directions for you to carry out. If your child is very young, you may need to show her the idea first—you can place your finger on your own nose and say, "See my nose? Now touch *your* nose." If your child is unable to do this, place her finger on her nose and say, "There's your nose." Continue playing the game as long as you both enjoy it.

VARIATION 1:   As you play this game, compare the sizes and shapes of various parts of the body. For example, you can put your hand or foot next to your child's and ask her to tell you how yours is different from hers. (This reinforces learning how to compare and contrast, as presented in Chapter 6—Mathematics.)

VARIATION 2:   Ask your child to close his eyes. Touch some part of his body, and let him tell you what part you touched. If this is too difficult, play the game first with your child's eyes open.

VARIATION 3:   You can play the game "Simon Says" as you and your child touch and name parts of the body. For example, "Simon says touch your knee." Your child is to follow the directions only when "Simon says" to do so. If you simply say, "Touch your knee," your child is supposed to do nothing, and wait for another "Simon says" direction.

VARIATION 4:   With a very young child you can play the old game of "Brow Bender, Eye Peeper." As you say the words, touch the body part mentioned.

Brow Bender (Touch your child's forehead)
Eye Peeper (Touch eyes)

Nose Dropper (Touch nose)

Mouth Eater (Touch mouth)

Chin Chopper (Tickle chin)

Activity 2 *"Wiggle Your Nose"*

*Touching and Naming Parts of the Body
(to coordinate auditory signals and the
movement of body parts)*

DIRECTIONS: Ask your child to sit on the floor. Explain that each time you call out the name of a body part, she is to move that part. If you alternate left and right, the game is more challenging (for example, "right foot," "left ear," "right eye"). Your child may also enjoy it if you start at the top of her head and move downward or start with her feet and work upward. Be sure to take turns with your child, letting her call out directions for you to follow.

VARIATION: As you play the game above, ask your child to tell you how the parts of her body are related to each other. For example, "My right knee is connected to my right foot," "My nose is connected to my face," "My thumb is part of my hand." (See also Activities 45, 97, 98, and 99)

Activity 3 *"Mittens on My Hands and Boots on My Feet"*

Matching Clothes to Parts of the Body, Getting Dressed

MATERIALS: The clothes your child will wear for the day.

DIRECTIONS: This activity is to be done as your child is dressing himself (with or without your help). As he puts on his clothes, ask him to name each piece of clothing and where it goes. For example, "My sock goes on my foot," "My pants go over my legs," "My sweater goes over my head, and the sleeves go on my arms."

VARIATION: *Materials:* Doll or large paper doll, doll clothing. Suggest to your child that he can dress one of his dolls, playing the game as described above. (See also Activity 10)

Activity 4   "Obstacle Course"

Controlling the Whole Body

MATERIALS: A ball of soft string.

DIRECTIONS: Arrange movable pieces of furniture to form an obstacle course. With the string hanging loosely, mark the path you want your child to take, passing the string over chairs, under a table, behind the couch. Then ask her to follow the string through the course. She may enjoy setting up a different obstacle course for herself to follow, or she might invite you to try the course.

Activity 5   "Give Me a Part, and I'll Make You a Person"

Relating Body Parts to the Whole Body

MATERIALS: Paper; crayon, pencil, or pen.

DIRECTIONS: Draw a specific part of the body—for example, a foot or an arm. Ask your child to complete the picture and make a whole person. Try it again, starting with a different part of the body. Then let your child draw a part so you can take your turn finishing the picture.

Activity 6   "Pretzels"

Learning to Control Parts of the Body in Motion

DIRECTIONS: Ask your child to sit on the floor. Give directions like the following: "With your right elbow, touch your left hand." "With your nose, touch your right knee." "With your left thumb, touch your right thumb." "With your left heel, touch the toes of your right foot." If any of these is too difficult, you can help by demonstrating. After doing a few of these, your child will enjoy making up similar "tricks" for you to attempt.

VARIATION: For fun with body sensations, ask your child to stretch, wrinkle his nose, squint his eyes, wiggle his toes, stand on tiptoes, clench his fists, breathe slowly, breathe fast, crawl on hands and knees, bend over and touch his toes, shake both wrists, bend his knees, make his arms go around like windmills, and anything else you can think of.

COORDINATING LARGE MUSCLES

Large-motor coordination involves the general physical coordination of the muscles of the legs and arms and overall body balance. By the time a child enters school, typical large-motor activities involve skipping, jumping, running, and calisthenics such as jumping jacks and walking a balance beam.

Few children have to be encouraged to perform activities that develop large-motor coordination. Much of it is natural and spontaneous. Just watch a child's face as she climbs, jumps, or runs. Listen to her pride in herself as she calls out, "Watch me! I can slide down the big slide!"

There is considerable variation in the large-motor abilities of young children. How well a child performs will depend on her particular timetable of development. Your child needs safe areas to explore, both indoors and outdoors. As with all motor skills, practice strengthens a child's ability to perform and also develops her sense of accomplishment and her confidence that she will be able to master more difficult tasks. Pleasure in being able to perform easily continues into the physical activities and sports of later childhood, adolescence, and adulthood.

Activities 8 and 13 involve a child's gaining control over her large muscles. Activities 7 and 19 relate a task to the control of large muscles. Activities 9 and 15 tie together oral directions with control of the body. Activities 11 and 17 work on developing balance and leg muscle control, and Activities 14 and 16 coordinate body balance with arm and shoulder strength and coordination. Activities 12 and 18 emphasize creative movement and the control of large muscles. Activities 20 and 21 ask the child to incorporate the skill of balancing into the control of her large muscles. Finally, Activity 10 combines the skills of large- and small-motor coordination in the game of "Dress Up."

Activity 7 "My Beautiful Balloon"

Batting a Balloon in the Air
(to develop large muscle coordination)

DIRECTIONS: Show your child how to keep the balloon in the air by batting it with the palms of his hands. See how long he can keep it in the air and prevent it from touching the floor. He will

also enjoy batting the balloon against a wall and can try to see how long he can keep it going without losing control of it.

Activity 8   *"I'm a Tree, You're a Rock"*

Making Different Forms and Shapes with the Body

DIRECTIONS: Show your child how to make different shapes with her body. She can make herself flat like a rug, round like a ball, humped up like a rock, tall and straight like a tree, big like a house. She will enjoy changing the shape of her body from one form to another.

Activity 9   *"Roly Poly"*

Controlling the Body in Motion

DIRECTIONS: First your child lies down on the floor, preferably on a rug. See if he can follow your directions such as "Roll over once, and end up on your back." "Roll over twice, and end up on your stomach." "Roll all the way across the room." You can vary the difficulty of the directions according to the age of your child. Your child will be delighted if you take his place on the floor and let him give you directions.

Activity 10   *"My Arms Go in My Sleeves"*

Combining Large and Small Muscle Movements

MATERIALS: Miscellaneous clothes which are too large for your child. (Castoffs are best.)

DIRECTIONS: In a box, collect a number of clothes such as hats, jackets, pants, dresses, pajamas, gloves, socks, boots, shoes. Give the box to your child and let her choose what she wants to put on. Offer help only if it is really needed. When your child has herself all dressed up, she will enjoy parading around and showing everybody. If your child is fairly young and still not sure of the names of different articles of clothing, be sure to mention the names or ask your child to say what they all are. (See also Activity 3)

Activity 11   *"Box Car Train"*

Stepping In and Out of Boxes
(to improve balance and leg muscle control)

MATERIALS: Several odd-sized cartons with tops removed, all chosen to be good sizes for your child to step into.

DIRECTIONS: You and your child arrange the boxes to form a somewhat crooked path across the room. Then ask your child to walk the path, or walk through the "box car train," stepping in and out of each box along the way. It will be more exciting if you do it, too. (See also Activity 133)

Activity 12   *"Space Ball"*

Making Patterns in the Air
(to improve grace and agility)

MATERIALS: A ball large enough for your child to hold easily in both hands.

DIRECTIONS: Show your child how to move the ball around in the air so as to make different patterns. You can call for a circle, square, figure eight, or any other shape. Take turns with your child and let him direct you to make different shapes.

Activity 13   *"No Hands, No Feet"*

Body Balancing

DIRECTIONS: Ask your child to sit on the floor with legs together and arms outstretched like the wings of an airplane. Tell her to raise both legs as high as possible, keeping her knees straight. See how long your child can balance on her buttocks without putting hands or feet down for support. Then have her slowly lower her arms and legs to the floor without tipping over.

Activity 14   *"Bean Bags"*

Balancing, Coordination of Arms

MATERIALS: Some beanbags.

DIRECTIONS: Your child will enjoy tossing beanbags into any convenient container—a pail, a large pan, a dishpan. She can stand closer to the target or farther away, according to her age and degree of coordination.

VARIATIONS: Your child also will enjoy doing the following with beanbags:

1. Tossing the beanbag into the air and catching it again.
2. Throwing the beanbag into the air and clapping hands before catching it.
3. Throwing the beanbag into the air and jumping before catching it.
4. Playing "Catch" with another person, tossing the beanbag back and forth and catching it. Older children can make this more challenging by standing farther apart.

Activity 15   *"Watch Me Go Fast, Watch Me Go Slow"*

Moving to Changes of Tempo

DIRECTIONS: Talk with your child about changes of tempo. Clap your hands at different speeds, and ask your child which is faster and which is slower. See if he can follow changes in the speed of your clapping as he walks around the room—sometimes slow, sometimes fast, and sometimes in-between. Then let him clap while you walk around. (See also Activity 98)

Activity 16 *"Junior Push-Ups"*

Pushing against the Wall
(to strengthen shoulder and arm muscles)

DIRECTIONS: Stand with your child about a foot from a wall, facing it. With elbows bent, lean toward the wall and push against the wall with both hands. Push yourself out from the wall, then lean against it. Move out and in several times, while your child does the same.

Activity 17 *"Jumping In, Jumping Out"*

Balancing and Controlling Leg Muscles

MATERIALS: A long piece of string, a rope, a clothesline, or some extension cords plugged together.

DIRECTIONS: Let your child make a pattern on the floor with the rope or string—for example, in the shape of a figure eight or two triangles or any other shapes. Let your child jump in and out of the spaces. Older children can try it hopping on only one foot. (See also Activity 117)

Activity 18 *"Duck for the Oyster, Dig for the Clam"*

Pantomime
(to control large muscles in a variety
of movements)

DIRECTIONS: Pretend you are sweeping the floor. Ask your child to guess what you are doing. Then let her act out some activity for you to guess. You and your child can take turns pantomiming things such as patting the dog or cat, shoveling snow, digging sand at the beach, kicking a ball, flying like a bird, ironing clothes, climbing a ladder, sawing wood, pounding nails, or anything else either of you can think of. (See also Activities 46 and 76)

Activity 19   *"Bounce and Catch"*

Improving Large Muscle Coordination
through Imaginative Movement

MATERIALS: A large ball.

DIRECTIONS: Ask your child to bounce the ball in front of him and catch it with both hands. When he can do this, ask him to bounce the ball a certain number of times and stop. As your child learns how to control the bouncing ball better, see if he can keep bouncing the ball, using only one hand each time. Finally, see if he can bounce the ball alternating right and left hands.

Activity 20   *"Straight and Narrow"*

Balancing and Control of the Body in Motion

DIRECTIONS: Whenever you and your child are out walking, encourage her to walk a straight, narrow line, both for fun and for balance. She can walk along a low wall or walk a straight line following the edge of the sidewalk. She can also follow a chalk line drawn on the garage floor or sidewalk, or you can lay down a long, narrow board somewhere outside the house and let her try to walk along the board without stepping off.

Activity 21   *"Balance the Books"*

Balancing Objects on the Head
(to improve balance and posture)

MATERIALS: Two books which you do not value very much, tied closed with string.

DIRECTIONS: Show your child how to balance one of the books on his head by demonstrating with the other book. When he can keep the book balanced as he stands still, encourage him to try walking slowly and carefully with the book still on his head. Once he learns to do this well, you can make the balancing more difficult by taping a strip of masking tape to the floor and asking him to walk this line, still carrying the book on his head. (See also Activity 133)

COORDINATING SMALL MUSCLES

The skills of reaching and grasping are usually defined as those of small-muscle or motor coordination. A key to successful small-motor coordination is the ability of the eye and the hand to work together. Watch a baby as he crawls along the floor. He can spot the tiniest object—a crumb, for example—and then use his thumb and index finger to pick it up. He is able to pick up individual pieces of cereal and put them in his mouth long before he can walk. Most children, by the time they are three or four years old, are fast learning to zip, snap, buckle, and button, especially if they have plenty of opportunities to practice. Other activities that are considered small-motor tasks are copying shapes, numbers, and letters as well as tracing, coloring, and tying shoelaces.

The need to develop skill in small-motor control is necessary for competence and success in almost everything we do as functioning adults. It has often been said that civilization as we know it would not exist were it not for humans' ability to pick up and grasp objects and otherwise use the hands as fine precision tools. Small-motor skills, such as brushing one's teeth, feeding oneself, and fastening one's clothes, provide the basis for self-help. They also enable a child to become more independent in just about everything she or he does, from learning how to write to driving a car.

Activities 22, 23, and 24 provide opportunities to improve finger and hand dexterity. Activities 25 and 27 reinforce the skill of eye–hand coordination. Activity 26 continues to emphasize finger dexterity but also includes the strengthening of fingers and hands. Activities 28, 29, and 30 combine finger dexterity, spatial awareness, and eye–hand coordination. Activity 31 incorporates the task of shoelace-tying into the skills of small-motor coordination.

Activity 22   "Poke, Push, Pound, and Pull"

Improving Finger Dexterity

MATERIALS: Newspapers or an old sheet, clay or other modeling material.

DIRECTIONS: Cover a table with newspapers or an old sheet. Let your child sit at the table and experiment with molding all sorts of shapes. He will not need any directions or help. This is an especially good activity for rainy days. Below are three different recipes for "play dough." Try them all and see which one you and your child like best. Vegetable coloring can be added to them or not, as you wish. All three recipes may be found in Doreen Croft's book, *Recipes for Busy Little Hands,* 585 No. California Avenue, Palo Alto, California 94301.

A.
1 cup flour
1/3 cup salt
1/3 to 1/2 cup water
1 teaspoon vegetable oil
(Add vegetable coloring to water if desired)

Mix flour and salt. Add water and oil gradually. If too stiff, add more water. If too sticky, add more flour. This can be used like clay, or can be flattened for making cutouts with cookie cutters. Store, covered, in the refrigerator.

B.
2 cups salt
1/2 cup cornstarch
water

Mix salt and cornstarch with enough water to form a paste. Cook and stir constantly over medium heat. Cool and store, covered, in the refrigerator. Less sticky than flour dough, and it keeps better because of its high salt content.

C.

2 cups salt	Heat salt and water together for 4 to
2/3 cup water	5 minutes. Remove from heat. Add
1 cup cornstarch	cornstarch and cold water (mixed
1/2 cup cold water	together) and stir until smooth.
	Cook over medium heat until thick.
	Store, covered, in refrigerator.

Activity 23   "I Am Making the Sun"

Using Tools, Developing Artistic Creativity

MATERIALS: Crayons or paint and brush, paper.

DIRECTIONS: Allow your child to draw or paint uninterrupted. If it pleases her, help her hang up her pictures for everyone to see. (See also Activity 107)

Activity 24   "Scrapbook"

*Cutting and Pasting, Making Pictures for a Scrapbook
(to combine a variety of small-motor activities)*

MATERIALS: Old magazines, old greeting cards, old catalogs, used postage stamps, yarn or ribbon, heavy paper, blunt scissors, paper punch (optional).

DIRECTIONS: Let your child draw or paint pictures to put in his scrapbook. He also will enjoy choosing pictures in magazines and catalogs to cut out and paste in his scrapbook. When he is satisfied that he has enough pages, punch holes in the pages and tie them together with yarn or ribbon to make a book. With young children this project can continue over a period of time. This is a good rainy day activity to keep your child and a friend or friends busy for an extended period of time.

Activity 25   "Splish Splash"

*Pouring and Measuring Liquids
(to promote eye–hand coordination)*

MATERIALS: A measuring cup, jars of various sizes, a funnel, paper, a pencil.

DIRECTIONS: At the kitchen or bathroom sink, let your child pour cupfuls of water into the various jars. You or she can record on the paper how many cups of water fit in each jar. (See also Activity 119)

Activity 26   *"Watch Me Do It with One Hand"*

Manipulating Small Objects with One Hand
(to promote hand and finger dexterity)

DIRECTIONS: Tear a sheet of newspaper into four pieces. Give one piece to your child and ask him to try to crumple it into a ball. Let him use his dominant hand, and explain that he cannot help with the other hand or push the newspaper against anything.

VARIATION: Put three or four coins or other small objects in your child's hand and ask him to hand them to you one at a time, in the order you ask for them. Older children can handle a larger number of objects at once.

Activity 27   *"Penny Pitching"*

Throwing Small Objects at a Target
(to strengthen eye–hand coordination)

MATERIALS: Six medium-sized bowls, baskets, or boxes; pennies or buttons.

DIRECTIONS: Arrange the six containers on the floor in two rows. Let your child pitch the pennies or buttons into the containers. When she has finished, she should count the number of pennies or buttons that have landed in each container. Your child can either do this by herself, or you can join her, taking turns with her. (See also Chapter Six and Activities 124 through 133)

Activity 28   *"Drop the Toothpick"*

Dropping Toothpicks through a Straw
(to develop finger dexterity and eye–hand coordination)

MATERIALS: Toothpicks, a drinking straw.

DIRECTIONS: Put a toothpick in your child's dominant hand and a drinking straw in the other. See if he can hold the toothpick at the level of his chin and drop it into the straw. If your child is very young, let him just fit the toothpick into the straw.

Activity 29   "Making a Necklace"

Stringing Beads
(to develop finger dexterity and eye–hand coordination)

MATERIALS: Macaroni or Cheerios, string, glue, blunt scissors.

DIRECTIONS: Ask your child to cut a piece of string the right length for a necklace. Next, dip one end of the string (about ½") into the glue. When the glue is dry, your child can use the hardened tip to string the Cheerios or macaroni. Necklaces also can be made with seeds, cranberries, or popcorn.

VARIATION: Let your child make a necklace by joining safety pins or paper clips to each other.

Activity 30   "Clothespin in the Bottle"

Dropping Clothespins into a Bottle
(to strengthen spatial awareness and increase
muscle control of hands and fingers)

MATERIALS: Clothespins (push-on type, not the clip-on type); plastic milk bottle, quart jar, or half-gallon milk carton cut off at the top.

DIRECTIONS: Show your child how to stand in front of the jar holding the clothespin at waist level with the head of the clothespin pointing down. She is to drop the clothespin and try to get it into the bottle. You can play the game, too, using another bottle, or taking turns with your child. Very young children can enjoy simply loading clothespins into a milk carton.

Activity 31   "One, Two, Buckle My Shoe"

Tying Shoelaces
(to solve a small-motor task for hands and fingers;
learning a sequence)

MATERIALS: A pair of shoes with laces, preferably shoes that fit your child.

DIRECTIONS: Remove the laces from the shoes, then help your child string the laces through the shoe eyelets so that they come out right. Teach her the first step toward tying her shoelaces: let her bring together the two ends of the lace and join them by putting one over and under the other. When your child can do this easily, show her the rest of the sequence, including the final bow knot. She will be very pleased when she can tie her own laces.

CHAPTER THREE

Listening and Hearing

Auditory perception is the awareness of sound in all its complexity—its direction, quality, pitch, volume, rhythm, and duration. Once sound has been sensed by the ear and perceived by the brain, it can be stored in the memory of the brain and kept available for future use.

Very often the newborn baby is startled by loud sounds and responds to these sounds by crying. In just a few weeks, though, as the baby becomes familiar with certain loud noises, she can tolerate these or even enjoy them, accepting them as a normal feature of the environment. The baby learns to organize clusters of sounds into concepts that make sense out of all the confusing stimuli reaching the ear. For example, the infant hears the sudden loud sound of the doorbell. The first time it seems like an alarming, isolated event. Later, she will piece together a familiar sequence that includes doorbell, footsteps, opening of the door, voices, closing of the door, and more footsteps. Another example: the infant hears water running in the bathroom and associates this sound with the enjoyment of her bath. Later, she can experience the same pleasure of anticipation simply from hearing her father's or mother's cluster of words, "It's time for your bath." Learning to group sounds of all kinds into patterns is an important step toward understanding words and sentences.

Two major aspects of auditory perception will be considered in this chapter—differentiating sounds (auditory discrimination) and remembering sounds (auditory memory). The activities are grouped accordingly.

DIFFERENTIATING SOUNDS

The ability to hear likenesses and differences in sound is called "auditory discrimination." The young child's world contains a bewildering collection of sounds—the hum of the vacuum cleaner, the swish of water in the washing machine, the creak of a door, the ticking of a clock, the barking of a dog, and the voices of people around him. Very early in life an infant learns to distinguish the voices of family members. A young child will help himself to differentiate between sounds by imitating and making his own sounds, trying to match them to the sounds he hears. He will happily imitate a car motor or a motorcycle revving up, and will delight in the sound effects he can make of an airplane taking

off. Talking and listening as he interacts with members of the family do a great deal for the young child's skill in auditory discrimination.

Activities in this section concentrate on distinguishing between different sounds in the environment, relating verbal messages to appropriate body responses, and helping a child achieve greater sensitivity toward sounds in terms of pitch, volume, rhythm, and word and sentence patterns. Activity 33 asks the child to identify various animal sounds, while Activity 34 identifies objects by the sounds they make. Activities 39 and 40 broaden a child's awareness of sounds and encourage a sensitivity to different kinds of sounds. Activity 32 makes a child aware of general rhythmic patterns, and Activity 38 is more specific in asking a child to give the names of particular melodies or songs after hearing them hummed or sung. Activity 36 actually provides the physical sensation of feeling sound, while Activities 35, 37, 41, and 42 develop more specifically an awareness of pitch, volume, quality, and rhythm. Finally, Activities 43, 44, and 45 begin to relate the skills of auditory discrimination to actual words or verbal commands, an important readiness step toward developing beginning reading skills.

Activity 32   *"Tap and Clap"*

Keeping Time to Music
(to strengthen ear–hand and ear–foot coordination)

DIRECTIONS: You and your child should first choose a song—for example, an easy, repetitive song like "Old MacDonald Had a Farm." Now you should both pat your knees with the palms of your hands to keep a steady beat going while you sing the song. Next you can sing the song over again, this time keeping the steady beat by tapping your feet.

VARIATION: You and your child can have fun clapping the rhythms of the names of family members or friends. For example, E-*liz*-a-beth, Pa-*tri*-cia, *Greg*-o-ry, *Grand*-dad-dy. (See also Activity 98)

Activity 33   *"It Sounds Like a Dog, or Maybe a Wolf"*

Distinguishing Animal Sounds

DIRECTIONS: You and your child can play a guessing game with sounds. Start with a sound very easy to identify—meowing like a cat or barking like a dog. Your child will enjoy imitating baby chicks, crows, cows, lions, pigs, goats, turkeys, and any number of interesting sounds.

VARIATION: You and your child can play with rhyming words. At first suggest a word like "hat" and ask your child how many other words she can think of that sound like "hat." Then let her give you a word for rhyming, and continue to take turns. (See also Activity 77)

Activity 34   *"Drop It and Call It"*

Identifying Objects by Sound

MATERIALS: A ball, a spoon, a penny, a pencil, a book, a plastic cup or dish; other objects that make a recognizable sound when dropped.

DIRECTIONS: Make a collection of objects similar to those listed above, and put them on a table. Let your child look at them. Then ask him to close his eyes. Drop one item on the floor and ask him to guess which item you dropped. Repeat until you have dropped all the items. You can make this activity more difficult by not showing your child the objects before dropping them.

Activity 35   "Pluck It"

Making and Playing a Rubber Band Guitar
(to reinforce sensitivity to pitch and resonance)

MATERIALS: A shoe box or stationery box, or any box in this size range, without a lid; rubber bands of different sizes and widths, large enough to fit around the box.

DIRECTIONS: Show your child how to stretch several rubber bands around the box, some large enough to be loose, some small enough to be tight; space them about an inch apart. He will be delighted to pluck at the rubber bands and notice the different sounds made by the different "strings" of the guitar.

Activity 36   "Comb Kazoo"

Hearing and Feeling Sound Vibrations

MATERIALS: A comb, a piece of waxed paper.

DIRECTIONS: Show your child how to fold a piece of waxed paper in half and place the teeth of the comb inside the fold. Then, ask her to place her lips over the fold and move the comb from side to side as she hums a tune. You and your child can take turns playing the comb kazoo and letting the other guess what the tune is.

Activity 37   "Musical Glasses"

Hearing Sounds with Different Pitches
(to increase sensitivity to pitch)

MATERIALS: 8 drinking glasses, water, a spoon.

DIRECTIONS: Pour water into each glass, starting with a small amount in the first glass and increasing the amount of water, glass by glass, so that you have the most water in the last glass. Show your child how to tap the glasses gently with the spoon to hear which ones sound higher in pitch and which sound lower. If you like, you can adjust the water levels to make a scale, so that you or your child can play simple tunes on the musical glasses.

Activity 38   *"Tell Me the Tune"*

Identifying Tunes
(to help recognize auditory patterns)

DIRECTIONS: Ask your child if she would like to play a guessing game with songs. Let her listen while you hum a tune or sing one without words. Then ask her to guess what song it is. She will enjoy taking turns singing or humming tunes to be identified. You can make this activity more difficult by singing or humming only a part of the song.

Activity 39   *"Crickets and Cows"*

Hearing the Sounds Around You
(to broaden the range of sounds perceived)

DIRECTIONS: Ask your child if he would like to play a game of seeing how many sounds he can hear. Let him close his eyes and listen carefully. He should tell you all the different sounds he hears—for example, a cricket chirping, a car passing, the wind in the trees, an airplane, a bird singing. You can add any sounds you hear that he missed. You can make a "sound collection" if you like. Keep adding new sounds to your list as you play the game on different occasions and in different places. (See also Activity 88)

Activity 40   *"Cock-a-Doodle-Do"*

Listening to Sounds of Birds and Insects
(to sharpen sensitivity to pitch, volume, rhythm,
and quality of sounds)

DIRECTIONS: When you go out for walks with your child, see how many birds and insects he can identify by the way they sound. He will easily learn those he hears most often and those that are very distinctive. Some of them might be crickets, cicadas, crows, katydids, roosters, robins, owls, seagulls, pigeons, mockingbirds, woodpeckers, whippoorwills, ducks, or wild geese. If your child gets in the habit of noticing the different patterns of sounds made by birds and insects, he will be interested to hear new ones when he is on a trip or visiting a new locality.

Activity 41   *"Buzzing and Booming"*

Describing the Nature of Sounds
(to heighten awareness of the quality of sounds)

DIRECTIONS: You and your child can play a game of trying to describe the quality of all the different sounds you hear. You can start with easy words like "loud" and "soft," then "high-pitched" and "low-pitched." Others might be "repeated," "in rhythm" (fast or slow), "long" (like a train whistle), "short" (like a sneeze), rasping, hissing, squeaking, thumping, scraping, screeching, whining, tooting, shouting, whistling, crashing, ringing, buzzing, banging, booming, grunting, snorting, snuffling, trickling, and as many more as you can think of.

Activity 42   *"Follow My Pitch"*

Hearing and Matching Pitches
(to increase sensitivity to sound frequencies)

DIRECTIONS: This is an activity you can do with your child almost anywhere—at home, on walks, driving in the car. You can sing or hum a single note and see if your child can match the pitch exactly. If she is too low, point your finger up, and if she is too high, point your finger down. Soon she will be able to correct her pitch to match yours without any signals from you. She will take pleasure in singing notes for you to match too. This activity will help your child learn to "carry a tune."

Activity 43   *"Sing a Song of Sixpence, a Pocket Full of Pie"*

Correcting Wrong Words
(to recognize incorrect words and reinforce memory)

DIRECTIONS: Ask your child if she would like to play a game of "right" and "wrong" words. Start by reading any poem, nursery rhyme, or story she knows well, and change some of the familiar words of the original to different, "wrong" words. For example, "Jack and Jill went up the mountain," or "Goldilocks and The Three Chairs." Your child will take great delight in correcting you and will lose no time in making up "wrong" versions for you to correct.

Activity 44   *"Hide the Thimble"*

Hiding and Seeking
(to follow directions from auditory messages)

MATERIALS: A small object such as a toy or thimble.

DIRECTIONS: Hide the object and then ask your child to start looking for it. As he gets nearer to the hiding place, say, "Hotter, hotter." As he moves away from the hiding place, say, "Colder, colder." As soon as your child finds the hidden object, he will want to hide it and give you the signals to find it.

VARIATION: Instead of saying "hotter" or "colder," you can clap your hands loudly for "hotter" and softly for "colder."

Activity 45   *"Hug That Tree"*

Giving Directions on a Walk
(to relate motor control to auditory messages)

DIRECTIONS: When you and your child go for a walk together, you can take turns giving each other instructions to carry out. For example, "Sit down on that wall," "Hug that tree," "Pick up the stick over there," "Walk through those leaves," "Skip up this hill," "Walk and sing at the same time." (See also Activities 2 and 58)

REMEMBERING SOUNDS

The ability to remember what one hears is called auditory memory. It is essential for speaking and for understanding what has been said. A child remembers sequences of words and the events associated with them. Long before she can talk herself, she is able to respond to the words of others and react appropriately. By doing so, she is demonstrating the usefulness of her auditory memory, which tells her she has heard the same cluster of words many times before.

Auditory memory is essential to building vocabulary and sentence structure as a child learns to use clusters of sounds and words. An example is a child's ability to repeat exactly a sentence she has heard or to modify it to suit her needs. If her mother says, "Joan, you have to go to bed now," a very young child will often repeat a cluster of words—"Go to bed now"; or, if she wants to question her mother's command, "Go to bed now?" A slightly older child will be able to create a more complete sentence perhaps by changing the original statement into a full question, "Do I have to go to bed right now?"

Activities 46 and 48 increase a child's ability to recall the details and sequence of a story, poem, song, or narration. Being able to retain key parts of word and sentence selections is an important characteristic in developing the ability to respond accurately and intelligently in oral dialogue. Activity 47 develops the skills involved in learning the alphabet or remembering one's telephone number. Activities 49 and 50 continue to strengthen the child's ability to retain bits of information and either remember the sequence of items presented or transmit them accurately; Activity 49 also emphasizes the creative aspect of composing one's own word and sentence patterns while adding onto another person's similar list.

Activity 46   *"Echo Story"*

Retelling a Story
(to strengthen memory of detail and sequence)

DIRECTIONS: Tell your child a familiar story (or read one to him). Ask him to tell it back to you. He may want to act out parts of the story as he tells it.

VARIATION: You can read or tell or make up the first half of the story and let your child finish it. Then he can repeat your first half, and let you repeat his last half of the story. (See also Activities 18, 63, and 76)

Activity 47   *"2-4-3/J-L-K"*

Recalling Sequences

DIRECTIONS: Call out a series of three numbers and ask your child to repeat them back to you in the same order. Use the same numbers in a different order, then use a new set of numbers. You can also use color names ("pink—blue—yellow") or letters of the alphabet in various orders. When your child can easily repeat three items correctly, increase the number to four and then to five. (See also Activity 144)

Activity 48   *"Jack Be Nimble, Jack Be Quick,*
Jack Jump over the Candlestick"

Memorizing Poems and Songs
(to teach retention of complete patterns
of words and notes)

DIRECTIONS: Read a poem or sing a song or a nursery rhyme to your child often enough so that she will be able to memorize it and be able to sing it or say it herself. Then you can clap the rhythm while she says it or sings it, and then she can clap while you say or sing verses. Many poems that are popular with young children may be found in various collections of Mother Goose or in *When We Were Very Young,* by A. A. Milne (author of the *Winnie the Pooh* books).

Activity 49 *"Grandmother's Trunk"*

Building a Story
(to remember a sequence of objects)

DIRECTIONS: This is an old game often called "Grandmother's Trunk." You can start by saying "I opened my grandmother's trunk, and I found a hat." Then your child takes her turn and she might say, "I opened my grandmother's trunk, and I found a hat and a mouse." Then you will add a third item to these two, and your child will add a fourth to the preceding three. You can continue as long as you like, always repeating the items already mentioned. Unlimited variations of this game are possible. You can say, "I'm going to visit Grandma, and I'm taking . . ." or "I went to the market and bought a . . ." or "I went on a picnic, and took . . ." or "I went to the zoo, and saw. . . ."

Activity 50 *"The Whispering Game"*

Receiving and Sending Messages
(to sharpen coordination of hearing and speech)

DIRECTIONS: Although you can play this game with your child, it is best played with several people. The players sit in a circle. The first person whispers a sentence into the ear of the person to the left of her. The second person whispers the sentence, exactly as she hears it, into the ear of the person to her left, and so forth around the circle. The last person repeats the sentence aloud, and the first person tells everybody what the original sentence was. Usually there is little resemblance between the two.

CHAPTER FOUR

Language

A child begins the fascinating, almost magical process of learning language soon after birth. It is exciting to see how an infant's coos, gurglings, mumblings, and cries of joy or wonderment lead, step-by-step, to words and language. At a very early age, a child begins to practice many skills essential for later ability to comprehend what is heard and read and to translate thoughts into spoken and written words. A child needs help in transforming a huge collection of random experiences into ideas he or she can understand and use. To make sense out of the infinite variety of processes, shapes, colors, textures, and sounds in the world, a child must learn to think about things in regular, predictable, orderly ways, classifying and sorting out the raw materials of day-to-day experiences.

At first, a child begins to play and experiment actively with sounds she or he hears, trying out vocalization capacity by babbling. Gradually, the child starts to imitate the same sounds and words their parents and caregivers are using. A child's first words are likely to be those that refer to close and intimate experiences— "Mama," "Dada," "cookie," "dog." A good deal of a child's language development happens spontaneously as a result of daily interactions with others. Still, there is much that can be done to strengthen and enrich language development. A child needs constant practice in learning to translate experiences into ever-more-logical thought patterns and eventually into discriminating choices of words, phrases, and sentences. A child must discover that he or she can use words to identify interesting ideas—not only tangible objects like "cup" and "table," but also sensory messages such as "hot," "wet," and "hungry." Adults take for granted the ability to distinguish green from red or right from left. A child, however, finds these distinctions mysterious before mastering such concepts. Often, stimulation or expansion is necessary to help a child grasp meanings.

One of the most important stimulations of language development is conversation between a child and other people. Simply taking the time to talk about topics of mutual interest helps build a good language base. The talking partners can be older siblings, friends in the neighborhood or at school, relatives, teachers, and, of course, parents. Studies have shown that it is the quality or substance of the conversations and not the quantity that is important. An adult's conscious elaboration and extension of simple discussions can help the child develop vocabulary and sentence structure.

Related to this is the *child-directed* speech that many adults use when talking with children. Many adults do, in fact, talk differently to children. Often, adults use shorter sentences, a higher pitch, increased modulation, simple vocabulary, speaking in the here-and-now, enhanced facial expression, and repetition of words and phrases. Most adults and even children do this spontaneously, always adapting to the linguistic level a little above where the child's language is. This helps simplify language and makes it easier to learn—children can pick out and hone in on the language meant for them. Adults should trust their natural impulse to talk to children in this way. While many claim they do not want to use baby talk or that they try to talk to children in an adultlike manner, adults should take heart that the natural instinct to speak to children in a specialized way is perhaps the greatest help given in language learning.

As presented in this chapter, the three important areas basic to early language development are language concepts, vocabulary and expression, and logical thinking. The three are closely related to each other. However, these language development areas are presented in separate sections for each reinforces a slightly different part of a child's language base.

LANGUAGE CONCEPTS

Most children learn very early that there are distinct and consistent symbols for various objects in our world. When your little one can point to a dog running by and shout "dog," you know that he has grasped an important idea—our language is but a symbolic image of the world as we know it. It is a convenient way to represent and communicate experience. The use of concepts is basic to a child's understanding of the world. The concept can be an object like a chair or an animal, or it can be an idea such as the difference between "in" and "out" or "rough" and "smooth."

Concept learning evolves gradually. Only through real experience and constant reinforcement by those around her can a child thoroughly come to understand a concept. For example, every time the cat walks by, the child's mother or father might say, "See the nice kitty?" or "Would you like to pet the cat?" Similarly, the father or mother refers to the dog as "dog" or perhaps "doggie." A young child usually becomes quite accurate in her ability to label

and differentiate objects around her. As a next step, the child learns the distinctions between *kinds* of dogs and *kinds* of cats. At this stage she will be able to distinguish between dog and puppy or yellow cat and black cat.

It would be easier for your child to master our language system at a relatively early age if he had to learn only the words for tangible objects. As mentioned above, however, we have many words that refer to ideas, such as "before" and "after," that a child cannot see or touch. When you are trying to define "after," your child might grasp it more easily if you contrast it with "before": before dinner-after dinner, before nap-after nap. As you show your child when and where "after" is appropriate, he begins to master another level of language use—the idea that words are good for intangible ideas as well as tangible objects.

Activities 51 and 59 reinforce the naming, labeling, and describing of objects for your child. Activity 52 demonstrates words used in action. Activities 53, 54, 55, and 56 deal with some basic concept words—"curved," "round," "straight," pairs of things, "back" and "front," and "small," "medium," and "large." Activities 57 and 60 continue to help acquaint a child with the "process words," showing relationships such as "on," "next," "above," "right," and "through." Activity 58 reinforces the idea of following a sequence of concrete ideas verbally, while Activity 61 helps illustrate the idea of possession. Activity 62, another approach to examining objects, explores the concept of different points of view—what does an object look like from various angles or vantage points?

Activity 51   "Walkie-Talkie"

Tour of the House
(to learn the names of objects)

DIRECTIONS: Take a trip around the inside of your house and see if your child can name everything you point to. This activity is good for a child's growing realization that everything has a name and that it is important to distinguish one thing from another. If your child has no difficulty with this activity, try distinguishing between things that have similar properties such as a bedspread and a quilt. Discuss the similarities and differences between the objects and the uses for each.

Note: This is also excellent for learning new words (see the next section in this chapter). In addition, you can try the activity on trips or when walking in the yard or around the block. To make this activity into a game, take turns, and let your child point to some things for you to name. This also will reinforce the names of things and their correct pronunciation.

Activity 52   "Seesawing"

Words that Show Action
(to teach the use of verbs)

DIRECTIONS: Explain to your child that some words express motion or action. For example, talk about children *seesawing* on the playground, point out the wagon *rolling* down the driveway or the dog *wagging* her tail. You might ask your child to think of some words that express action, so that either one of you (or both of you at once) can act them out. Finding action words in favorite stories or collections of poems, such as the tales of Mother Goose, leads to many imaginative possibilities (for example, "London Bridge is *falling* down").

Activity 53   "What Shape Is It?"

Learning about Different Kinds of Shapes
(to distinguish among curved, round, and straight)

MATERIALS: Miscellaneous kitchen utensils.

DIRECTIONS: Find items in your kitchen that are curved, round, or straight such as a mixing bowl, frying pan, knife, fork, soup can, spoon. Ask your child to group the items you and he select according to the shape of each. If your child has difficulty with the idea of "curved," you may want to limit your collection at first to round and straight items.

Activity 54   "Just Alike"

Learning about Pairs of Things

MATERIALS: Old magazines or catalogs for cutting out objects that are pairs.

DIRECTIONS: Show your child objects that are paired such as mittens, socks, candlesticks, salt and pepper shakers. Ask her to find some pairs on her own. You can also illustrate pairs by collecting pictures of pairs of items from an old catalog or magazine that your child can cut up. (This is also good for small-muscle coordination.)

Activity 55   "Front and Back"

Distinguishing Back from Front

MATERIALS: Paper or newspaper (optional).

DIRECTIONS: Children often have difficulty remembering the difference between back and front. Beginning with your child's own body, you might want to help him point out which is his front and which is his back. Toes and heels are also good for learning front and back. Then, move to items in his immediate environment such as the front of the house and the back of the house. You can also talk about the front and back of the car, a chair, a shelf. For fun, you can ask your child to write his name on the front of something you do not mind marking up (like a piece of paper or a newspaper), and then have him draw a design or picture on the back.

Activity 56   *"Family of Jars"*

Exploring "Small," "Medium," "Large"
(to introduce sequence)

MATERIALS: Plastic bottles or jars of different sizes and shapes, and their lids.

DIRECTIONS: Ask your child to line up the bottles or jars in order of size and place the appropriate lid on each one of them. She may need your help. Point out different containers, and show how one is bigger or smaller than another. Show your child how the smallest are at one end, the medium-sized ones in the middle, and the largest at the other end. Taking off the lids and putting them on again reinforces the idea of relative sizes and also helps develop small-muscle coordination in the fingers. As a good follow-up activity, read "Goldilocks and the Three Bears" or "The Three Billy Goats Gruff." Emphasize the comparative sizes of the porridges, bowls, bears, chairs, beds, or goats. (See also Activity 114)

Activity 57   *"Put It on the Table"*

Setting the Table
(to follow instructions and understand
words showing relationships)

MATERIALS: A table, plates, glasses, placemats, silverware, salt and pepper shakers.

DIRECTIONS: Place the above items near your kitchen or dining room table. Ask your child to help you and give him the following instructions.

1. Put the placemats *on* the table, one for each person.
2. Put the plates *on* the placemats.
3. Place one knife to the *right* of each plate.
4. Place one spoon to the *right* of each knife.
5. Place one fork to the *left* of each plate.
6. Place one glass on the table *above* each knife.
7. Put the salt and pepper shakers in the *center* of the table.

Instead of the items above, substitute, if you like, the ones you use most frequently in setting the table. An activity such as this reinforces for your child the concept of idea words that express relationships or connections between objects.

VARIATION 1:

"Up and Down, Over and Under"

Materials: Flashlight (optional).

Directions: Children love to work flashlights. Give your child a working flashlight, and show her how to blink it on and off. Then ask her to blink it a specified number of times *between* two chairs, *over* the couch, *beside* the lamp, *in front of* the stove, *down* at the floor, *through* the door, while walking *around* a table, and *before* or *after* she sits down or stands up. Such an activity also reinforces your child's ability to identify objects around the house. In asking for a certain number of blinks, you are also introducing the idea of number (See Chapter 6—Mathematics). If you do not have a flashlight handy, let your child point at various locations and stamp her foot a certain number of times instead of blinking the light.

VARIATION 2:

"Where Is the Treat?"

Materials: A container and a nutritious food treat your child likes.

Directions: Show your child the following relative positions between the container and the treat: in/on; in front of/behind; close/far away; inside/outside. Use other positions that come to mind. Ask your child to tell you each time where the treat is in relation to the container. After your child has played this game, let him eat the treat (if it is still edible!). You also can use a penny, paper clip, or bottle cap instead of the treat, and a cup or small box as a container. For variety, you might want to take turns giving directions. This is excellent practice for your child not only in receiving directions but in giving them as well.

VARIATION 3:

"The Rope Circle"

Materials: Clothesline or string, about six or seven feet long.

Directions: Make a circle of the length of clothesline or string on the ground or on the floor of a large room. Suggest that your child "stand on the circle," "stand near the circle," "hop over the circle," "stand outside the circle." Later your child can identify for himself the positions he takes on the rope circle.

VARIATION 4:

"Swing *on* the Swing, Slide *Down* the Slide"

Directions: Take your child to a playground. Using the playground equipment as an obstacle course, call out directions such as "Jump *on* the merry-go-round," "Slide *down* the slide," "Crawl *through* the pipe," "Run *around* the swings." You can use any of the equipment available at your local playground, with directions of your own choosing.

Activity 58   *"You Say It, I Do It"*

Following Directions
(to listen carefully in following a sequence)

DIRECTIONS: Help your child follow directions. You can give either simple ones such as "Please put the paper on the table," or a more complicated sequence that involves a series of directions. For example, you can ask your child to touch her toes, hop around the chair, crawl on her hands and knees over to the window, and count how many cars she sees going by. There are any number of activities you can make up that will reinforce body control, direction, memory, large-muscle coordination, and other skills. Any sequence of directions involving your child's response to her own body parts and objects around the house are excellent developmental tasks. Your child will enjoy making up directions for you to follow as well. (See also Activity 45)

Activity 59   *"Pig in a Poke"*

Exploring Objects
(to use color, weight, and other sensory concepts)

MATERIALS: Any three objects you or your child chooses, plus a paper bag.

DIRECTIONS: Place the three objects in the paper bag. Let your child handle each one without looking into the bag. Ask him the following questions:

1. How does it feel? (smooth, rough, scratchy, sticky, soft)
2. What shape is it? (long, short, square, round, jagged)
3. What size is it? (large, small)
4. Can it make a noise? If the item does not produce a noise by itself, try hitting it against something else.
5. What do you do with it? What is it used for?

(See also Activity 111)

Activity 60 "All Around the Paper"

Exploring a Page
(to distinguish top, middle, bottom, shape, left/right, big/small, colors)

MATERIALS: A blank sheet of paper, crayons.

DIRECTIONS: There are many useful concepts you can develop with a sheet of paper by asking your child to follow these directions:

1. Fold the paper in *half* the long way.
2. Write your name on the *left* side and draw a picture on the *right* side.
3. Draw a *row* of circles or squares at the *top* of the page in any color you like. Draw another row of patterns in a different color at the *bottom* of the page.
4. Draw a *big* circle of some color in the *middle* of the paper.
5. Draw *small* circles around the borders of the *back* of the page.

You might want to change places with your child and have her give you directions, as you find the parts of the paper.

Activity 61 "Mine and Yours"

Showing Possession

DIRECTIONS: "Mine" versus "someone else's" is not a concept a child readily understands. For a young child it is natural and normal to assume that an object he wants is his. The idea of possession gradually comes as the concept of self evolves (see Chapter 8—Social and Emotional Development).

Pick an object that belongs to your child and compare it to an object that belongs to someone else. Discuss with your child the difference between "mine," "yours," and "theirs." By discussing with your child that his doll or truck "belongs to" him but that his friend's doll or truck "belongs to" his friend, you will not only help him understand the idea of ownership, but you may also be heading off potential sources of conflict.

Activity 62 *"Look at It Change When I Move"*

Developing Points of View
(to show how objects change or look different according to where you stand)

MATERIALS: An object that is interesting to talk about—for example, blocks, a book, a toy, or a favorite object belonging to your child.

DIRECTIONS: Put the object on the table. Ask your child to stand next to the table and look at the object. Now have her stand on a chair seat or stepstool and look down at the same object, or sit on the floor and look up at the object. Discuss with her how or why the object looks different depending on where you sit or stand. Do the objects change or do you change? Even though your discussion may only scratch the surface, you are introducing your child to the important concepts of perspective and individual point of view.

VOCABULARY AND EXPRESSION

A child will be able to use a new word as soon as he or she can see how the word relates to an understandable experience. This comes about through constant reinforcement of the relationship between the word and the experience. Even though a child can speak a particular word, he or she may not always be able to use that word correctly; it becomes firmly rooted in consciousness only when the word is used over and over again in concrete situations, with its various shades of meaning and impact on other people.

Conversation and informal talk with a child encourages a real understanding of language.

Vocabulary can be developed by taking trips with your child. Even during routine shopping expeditions to the local supermarket, a child will see new objects and learn new words. Whenever something new and different is seen, a child will ask questions about it and try to make sense out of it. Make sure he or she understands new words you use as you answer questions. It helps to associate the new word with a word a child already understands.

The activities in this section involve the use of new and old words with your child, in a variety of familiar and unfamiliar situations. The activities revolve around two major goals:

1. Helping your child realize that words have an important purpose in helping people communicate with each other.
2. Helping your child see that words affect those who hear them.

Activities 63 and 69 reinforce skills important for reading and writing. Activities 64, 65, 66, 68, and 70 involve the use of vocabulary words to describe, compare, and contrast items in your child's environment. Activity 75 reverses the procedure by providing the definition and asking your child to guess what the word is. Activities 71 and 72 encourage free talking and discussion with your child, while Activity 73 provides more structure by suggesting topics for discussion. Activity 67 asks your child to name occupations and also to describe them. Activities 76 and 77 promote the creative use of words in building vocabulary. Activities 73 and 74 reinforce vocabulary building with games that explore words that are both similar and opposite to each other.

Activity 63   "I'll Read You a Story"

Reading to Your Child
(to hear and see words used in books)

MATERIALS: Picture-story books.

DIRECTIONS: Read to your child often. She will enjoy hearing her favorite stories over and over again. Encourage her to talk about the stories and the pictures. Make comments while reading the book and ask her questions about what the two of you see. You can take turns reading books to each other. A young child may not

be able to recognize words in a book, but she enjoys telling the story as she follows the pictures. This is an excellent prereading exercise, for it teaches the child how a book should be read.

Mother Goose is a wonderful source of well-known rhymes and jingles for children. There are also many other picture books and picture-story books that reflect children's interests and develop prereading skills. For a list of books and magazines you can order, see Chapter Eight, Activity 186. Also, many can be borrowed from a local library. A good reference that offers guidelines and suggests books you can read with your child is *A Parent's Guide to Children's Reading* by Nancy Larrick, published by Bantam Books, Inc., 666 Fifth Avenue, New York, NY 10019.

VARIATION 1:
Encourage your child to tell you stories. These can be the retellings of stories you have been reading or they can be made up on the spot. Often, a story you tell will provide the stimulation for a child to continue the story or to begin a new one on his own.

VARIATION 2:
Dictate stories that your child tells you and then read them back so she can see that her spoken words have a written equivalent. Come back to it later to show that the words you wrote always retain the same meaning. Also encourage her to read what she had said.

VARIATION 3:
During mealtimes try to share experiences, ask questions about the day's events and activities, report on an interesting happening, talk about new places or events, or plan for some activity or trip with your child. (See also Activity 186)

Activity 64   "What Is It Made Of?"

Using Words to Describe Composition of Objects
(to develop language discrimination)

DIRECTIONS: Take a walk around the house with your child and touch all the things made of plastic, then wood, then glass, metal, leather, and rubber. Ask him to describe the objects to you—how they look, feel, and smell. You could also take a "color walk"—find all things that are green, red, orange, blue, or any other color you choose. In addition, you might want to combine two properties of one item. For example, ask your child to find all the brown things that are made of wood. This activity also emphasizes classification skills, which are important to mathematical reasoning (see Chapter 6—Mathematics).

VARIATION: Have your child think of the names of objects that belong in specific categories. For instance, have her list animals, foods, things that run on gasoline, glass items, appliances, letters of the alphabet, things with wheels. (See also Activities 88 and 89)

Activity 65   "Sweet and Sticky"

Describing Objects
(to use descriptive words)

DIRECTIONS: Choose an object and take turns with your child thinking of all the different words you can use to describe it. For instance, you could say "the *blue* car" and then have your child describe it in another way—"the *fast* car." Honey is sticky and sweet. A table is round, smooth, and cool. Other objects you can name to stimulate description are ice cubes, mud, toast, soap, fur, sand, rocks, sea shells, and many common household items. A slightly more demanding version is to have each of you repeat all the previous qualities listed for the object before giving yours. Your child will probably take great delight in repeating all the previous descriptions every time it is her turn.

VARIATION: Have your child close her eyes, handle an item, and describe how it feels.

Activity 66   *"Oranges and Bananas"*

Describing and Comparing Common Objects
(to encourage descriptive language)

MATERIALS: A banana and an orange, or any two fruits.

DIRECTIONS: Show your child the two fruits and ask him to tell you everything he can observe about them. Discuss how the two are alike and different. You can talk about the smell and taste as well as the appearance, color, weight, and so on. After you have finished looking at them, share the fruits as a nutritious snack. (See also Activity 111)

Activity 67   *"Policeman, Fireman"*

Naming the Occupation
(to hear and describe what people do for a living)

DIRECTIONS: Describe a certain type of work to your child and ask her to name the occupation of the people who do this work. For example: This man fixes cars ("mechanic"). This woman checks your teeth ("dentist"). This man delivers the mail ("mailman"). Reverse the procedure and see if your child can provide some job descriptions so that you can guess their occupations.

Activity 68   *"I'll Tell You about the Picture"*

Describing a Picture
(to help organize words into sentences; to convey
meanings and opinions to an audience)

MATERIALS: An old magazine with pictures that can be removed.

DIRECTIONS: Have your child cut out a picture (or cut one out for him), and have him tell you all about it. Describe what is happening, who or what is in the picture, what his feelings are about it, what he likes best or least about the picture, and what he thinks happened just before or just after the events depicted.

Activity 69   *"Save a Word"*

Reinforcing Words, Letters, and Numbers
(to emphasize prereading and writing skills)

DIRECTIONS: Point out and identify letters, words, and numbers in the environment whenever possible. Encourage your child to copy words or letters from book titles, soap boxes, telephone books, magazines, or any printed source where letters or numbers are found. You can establish a word bank for your child. On large-sized cards or pieces of cardboard, print out words she wants to save. You can simply ask your child to give you some of her favorite words or words she wants to keep.

Store the cards in a common box or on a shelf accessible to your child. Keep adding ones she does not know. Periodically, review the cards with your child and have her duplicate some of the words, if possible, either on a separate sheet of paper or by tracing over your existing letters (you can use tracing paper for this). Exhibit the words periodically. Shuffle them or have her go over them with friends if she would like to. See if she can begin recognizing some of the words by sight. Discard words she no longer wants. Keep the process spontaneous and free from pressure. (See also Activity 109)

Activity 70   *"Where I Went and What I Saw"*

Describing What You See
(to stimulate vocabulary growth)

DIRECTIONS: Before you travel anywhere, talk over with your child the purpose of the trip and what you and he can expect to see. Even a trip to the post office or the bank can be talked about before you go. Each trip should be discussed after you come back. Try to get your child to describe fully what he saw and how he felt about it.

Activity 71   "What Happened Today?"

Talking about the Day
(to use words and sentences in description and summary)

DIRECTIONS: Encourage your child, during dinner or at bed-time, to tell you some of the things about her day that she would like to share. They can be things she did or saw, something that happened to her, a description of an item she drew or built, something about her friends, her feelings about the way someone treated her, or a general overview of the day's events. This time is also a good opportunity to answer any questions your child might have stored up during the course of the day. Questions have a way of coming out if you encourage a quiet moment or a time for reflection with your child. It can be one of the best parts of the day for both of you. (See also Activities 137 and 190)

Activity 72   "Topic Talk"

Using Words in Familiar Contexts

DIRECTIONS: Think of a topic you and your child might enjoy discussing, and talk with him about the subject. Include a few words new to your child as you talk. Listed below are samples of topics you might choose.

1. Foods—what your child likes; different ways to cook foods; kinds of food (for example: meat, fish, vegetables, fruits, grains, nuts); types of food different animals or birds like to eat.

2. Activities your child enjoys during the various seasons of the year; what he likes to do on vacation trips, on walks, on picnics; special expeditions he likes such as visits to the aquarium, airport, or zoo.

3. Favorite toys—what the child does with them, why she likes them.

4. Things that move, or things that make sounds—cars, animals, water, bells, hammers, the wind blowing.

5. Imagining—for example, asking your child what he thinks it would be like to be a cloud, a kitten, or a bee.

6. Pets your child has or would like to have, how you care for them, what you feed them, what they like to do.

7. Things your child would like to make and how she would go about making them.

8. The kinds of clothing your child wears when it rains, when it snows, when it is hot, when he goes to the beach to swim, when he goes to a party.

9. An approaching holiday—which one it is, what your plans are for celebrating it, and how your child can help prepare for it.

Activity 73   "Some Like It Hot, Some Like It Cold"

Opposites
(to use words that are opposite in meaning)

DIRECTIONS: Suggest a word to your child and have her give its opposite. Then reverse the procedure—have your child give you a word and you suggest the opposite. This can be played by all members of the family at dinner or on a trip.

Activity 74   "Needles and Pins"

Synonyms and Shades of Meaning
(to use words that are similar in meaning)

DIRECTIONS: Explain to your child that many words in our language mean about the same thing: short-small-tiny; cold-icy-freezing. Give your child three words and have him choose the two that are similar in meaning. For example: big-large-man, or carton-ball-box. Provide your child with one word and see if he can think of words with similar meanings.

Activity 75   "Guessing Game"

Stimulating Word Pictures
(to create word imagery through description of objects)

DIRECTIONS: Describe to your child certain objects or events without actually naming them. Have your child guess what they are. For example:

1. The object I am thinking of has three wheels. It goes uphill or downhill when you pedal it.
2. I am thinking of an animal that stands in a field and eats grass.
3. This is something that lights up the sky at night and makes a loud noise.
4. When people use this plaything they climb to the top and go down faster than they went up.

Activity 76   "I Want to Be the Wolf"

Play-Acting
(to use creative language and to respond
creatively to language)

DIRECTIONS: Dramatize simple stories and nursery rhymes, with each member of the family taking a part. Good examples of rhymes to be used are "Little Miss Muffet," "Little Jack Horner," "The Three Little Kittens," "Humpty Dumpty," and "Jack and Jill." Children love to act out events and happenings. Adults call it play, but it is much more than that. Children are capable of improvising, pantomiming, and using puppets. They can and do relive events by acting them out.

Some stories suitable for play-acting are "The Little Red Hen," "The Gingerbread Boy," "Little Red Riding Hood," "Hansel and Gretel," "The Three Billy Goats Gruff," "The Three Little Pigs," "Goldilocks and the Three Bears," "The Pot That Would Not Stop Boiling," and "Chicken Little." Your child also might delight in acting out recent occurrences in the news such as a space walk or a sports event. Acting out a telephone conversation that did take place or might take place between the child and a favorite relative or friend is another activity that children enjoy a lot.

Note: Creative drama is also an excellent activity at birthday parties. (See also Activities 18 and 46)

Activity 77   "Fly on the Ceiling"

Making Up Silly Jingles
(to use words creatively)

DIRECTIONS: With your child, make up silly, nonsensical lines such as "A fly on the ceiling said, 'How are you feeling?' "

Your sentences do not necessarily have to rhyme and can be absolutely crazy. Children love to use words in original, off-beat ways. That is why children delight in saying and singing the Mother Goose rhymes. Playing with language also illustrates its power and effectiveness and stimulates the imaginative use of words and phrases.

VARIATION: You can start a sentence and have you and your child take turns adding one word at a time to the sentence. For example, you might start by saying "dogs," your child might add "are," you can add "furry," and so on until you jointly produce a complete sentence. (See also Activity 33)

LOGICAL THINKING

Logical thinking is continually developed through a child's daily interaction and contact with the environment and with the people closest to her or him. You can help your child make sense out of experiences, and you can encourage her or him to think and speak in a clear, orderly way.

Inquiry, which comes from a child's innate curiosity about the world, and the ability to understand what is happening are at the heart of clear thinking. As an example, a child's questions about Santa Claus and the Tooth Fairy may be attempts to sort out the difference between what is real and not real. Similarly, a child's apparent confusion about such ideas as cause and effect reveals a struggle to make sense out of the environment. It is not uncommon for a young child to think that the moving leaves on trees are causing the wind to blow.

Children grow intellectually by receiving constant, encouraging feedback and response from those around them. You can support their capacity for thought by helping children use words and ideas that satisfactorily express their view of moment-to-moment happenings. Try to answer all questions clearly and briefly. As you probably know already, this can be more difficult than it appears. How do you explain to your child why the sky is blue or what a thunderclap is? However, any attempt at explanation will help children make sense out of the often meaningless, buzzing tumult and confusion around them. Volunteering information or point-

ing out interesting happenings will further encourage children to think and reason about the world. Children will be able to transfer intuitively the language and thought skills they learn in these situations to the new, different, more complex experiences they will face in the future.

As you use the activities in this section, you will be talking with your child about everyday experiences and enriching their meaning. By wondering, questioning, generalizing, elaborating, and concluding with your child, you will be helping work through the complexities of the world.

Activity 80 challenges a child to think imaginatively of several different ways in which objects can be used. Activities 78 and 82 emphasize thinking and responding in complete sentences. Activities 79 and 81 stimulate logical thinking and the completion of unfinished sentences, while reinforcing cause and effect. Activity 84 encourages the development of thinking in logical thought patterns, while Activities 86 and 87 develop two different kinds of reasoning. Finally, Activities 83 and 85 promote creative problem solving.

Activity 78   *"Questions and Answers"*

Thinking in Complete Sentences
(to encourage the use of complete sentence patterns)

DIRECTIONS: To help your child learn to think and speak in complete sentences, you can play a game where one person asks the other a question. The person being asked cannot answer with only one word like "yes" or "no." For example, you can ask your child, "Is it raining today?" and he must respond with a complete thought such as "It was raining but now the sun is shining," or "Yes, it is raining harder and harder" (the word "yes" is part of the complete sentence).

Activity 79   *"Does a Pigeon Bark?"*

Logical Thinking
(to stimulate and reinforce logical thought patterns)

DIRECTIONS: The following absurd questions provoke the development of logical thinking and verbal expression in your child . . . and laughter, too.

1. Does a bird have fur?
2. Do we use a knife when we eat soup?
3. Do we put peanut butter on meat?
4. Do we eat pudding on a plate?

Just about any question (even one that is not absurd) that is understood by your child will stimulate her thinking processes. Try to select topics close to her own experiences that will appeal to your child. Taking the time to respond to questions your child asks naturally every day will further stimulate her thinking and her ability to reason.

VARIATION: You and your child can take turns making up statements that are nonsense. One of you talks nonsense, and the other corrects the statement. For example:

1. The kitty barks.
2. The cow blows her horn.
3. The lion squeaks.
4. The sun rises at bedtime.

Activity 80   *"How Shall I Use It?"*

Expanding on Uses of Objects

DIRECTIONS: Ask your child questions such as the following: What is the most important thing about . . .

> a plate? (You can eat from it)
>
> a door knob? (You can open a door with it)
>
> a bottle? (You can keep liquids in it)
>
> a nail? (It holds things in place)
>
> a straw? (You can sip drinks through it)

This is a very beneficial exercise, and the list of things about which you can ask your child is endless. We take for granted much that our children find strange. It helps to ask ourselves constantly, "How does my child view this object or event, and how can I help him perceive it more accurately?"

VARIATION: Ask your child to think of two or three ways to use kitchen chairs, a bathtub, a table, various items of furniture or playground equipment. You can reverse the procedure by asking your child to think of something and describe to you three ways it is used. Then you guess what "it" is. This is a good exercise for getting your child to speak clearly and informatively.

Activity 81   *"Because"*

Finishing Incomplete Thoughts
(to learn how to complete unfinished sentences)

DIRECTIONS: Ask your child to complete sentences like the following:

1. We could not play ball because _____.

2. The children were sad because _____.

3. John lost his hat because _____.

4. Everyone liked Judy because _____.

Keep making up new sentences as long as you and your child want to play, or ask her to think of sentences for you to complete.

Activity 82   *"Why"*

Responding with Complete Thoughts
(to encourage reasoning ability)

DIRECTIONS: Encourage your child to answer with a sentence when asked a question. Ask him questions that begin with the word *why*. Examples of questions are:

1. Why do we sleep?
2. Why do houses have windows?
3. Why do we wear woolly clothes in winter?
4. Why do we go to school?

It is good to let him ask you questions so you can model for him some complete sentences. (See the next activity for a closely related follow-up exercise.)

Activity 83   *"Color My Eggs Green"*

Imaginative Thinking
(to stimulate creative thinking)

DIRECTIONS: Have your child imagine some extreme situation. Ask her what would happen if:

1. There were no more water in the world.
2. People had wings.
3. There were no roads.
4. Birds did not have feathers.
5. Animals could talk.
6. Rocks could move themselves.
7. Houses had no windows.
8. It began to rain flowers.
9. People could walk on the ceiling.
10. The sun never set.

Activity 84 *"How Do You Do It?"*

Using a Logical Sequence to Accomplish Something

DIRECTIONS: Think of a process that requires a number of steps for its completion and ask your child, "How do you _____?" Examples would be the steps involved in making a sandwich, planting a garden, buying groceries, and cleaning up the house (a good one to work on!).

Activity 85 *"What Would You Do?"*

Problem Solving
(to encourage the application of workable solutions to selected problems)

DIRECTIONS: Present a situation to your child for him to solve. Accept any reasonable answer. The following are sample problems:

1. You accidentally knock over one of your mother's flower-pots as you run through the house. What would you do?
2. You could not find one of your mittens when it was time to go to school. What would you do?
3. Your baby brother starts crying because he bumped his head and your mother is talking on the telephone. What would you do?

Let your child present you with problem situations, too, for you to solve.

Activity 86 *"What Are You Thinking Of?"*

Moving from the General to the Specific
(to practice deduction from word clues)

DIRECTIONS: Either you or your child begins the game by making a statement such as "I am thinking of a bird," or "I am thinking of a thing that is square." The other person asks questions in an attempt to identify what her partner has in mind. Questions can be about color, size, shape, location, or any other likely key.

For example, "Is your bird black?" or "Is it very large?" The game is good for logical progression of ideas and for moving from one clue to the next.

Activity 87   "What Would You Say?"

Giving Appropriate Answers
(to develop the ability to generalize)

DIRECTIONS: Ask your child to respond to questions like the following: What would you say if you . . .

1. Wanted to stay overnight with a friend?
2. Wanted to go to the park with a friend?
3. Wanted to keep a baby kitten?
4. Spilled a glass of water on the bathroom floor?

CHAPTER FIVE

Looking and Seeing

Infants are able to see at birth. However, making sense out of what they see is a lifelong challenge. The process of receiving and interpreting visual stimuli is known as visual perception. Almost everything a child does involves visual perception—eating, using dishes and utensils, dressing, entering and leaving a room, playing with toys, patting the dog or cat, simply looking out the window.

A child, through visual perception, gradually learns to identify objects and distinguish one object from another. She learns that certain structures are called "doors" and others are called "windows." She learns that a car is bigger than a bicycle and that both are bigger than she is. She also learns that there are different shapes in her environment—a ball is round, a bed is rectangular, and a Christmas tree is triangular. When your child goes to school, accurate visual perceptual abilities will enable her to learn to read, write, spell, do arithmetic, and accomplish any other work involving the recognition and reproduction of visual symbols.

Because research has shown that maximum development of visual perception occurs roughly between the ages of three and eight, there is much you can do with your child at home to establish proficiency in visual perception. As your child helps you with everyday activities, such as sorting laundry, he will be sharpening his visual perception. At the same time he will be learning to assume responsibility around the house (see also "Assuming Responsibility" in Chapter 8). Many activities that help develop visual perception are also excellent for reinforcing basic mathematical principles (see Chapter 6). For example, sorting the laundry can help your child develop classification and comparison skills, as you both arrange the clothes according to color or size or type of article.

There are several areas important to visual perception and visual discrimination that gradually emerge out of the earliest consciousness of raw visual stimuli. Included in this chapter are activities centered on the areas of color recognition, differentiation of shapes, the difference between left and right, and alphabet recognition.

RECOGNIZING COLORS

Color is everywhere we look—in nature, houses, food, clothes, people. Colors are used for many things—they contribute to traffic safety—red for stop and green for go—and guide people to certain

areas of public buildings or supermarkets. Many parents teach their children colors without realizing that color recognition can help a child in early attempts to read. Beginning reading books often refer to colors in the text and use the corresponding colors in the illustrations ("See the cat chase the red ball" or "Go and ask the brown dog"). It is during the preschool years that most children learn the six basic colors—red, blue, yellow, orange, green, and purple. Some children as young as two years of age can identify familiar objects by colors, especially if parents keep referring to colors. For example, "You'd better wear your warm blue jacket today" or "Do you know where your other red sock is?"

It is not necessary to push color identification with your child. As with so many other concepts, she will learn this one when she is ready. Children are attracted to bright, clear colors. You can use them in your child's room and around your house to give pleasure and stimulation. Even very young infants enjoy colorful mobiles hung above their cribs.

Activity 88 reinforces a child's general sensitivity to any and all colors. Activity 89 focuses on specific items, in this case distinguishing the colors of different fruits and vegetables. Activities 90 and 92 turn to common color categories and ask a child to begin using judgment in matching colors in both real and game situations. Activity 91 explores the properties of colors and shows how selected choices of dyes can produce different color combinations.

Activity 88   *"Rainbow Walk"*

Taking a Walk and Observing Colors
(to identify colors in the environment)

DIRECTIONS: Take a "color walk" with your child. Talk ahead of time about all the colors of the rainbow, and suggest that you should both see how many colors you can find on your walk. You can do this in different seasons of the year and point out how the colors change with the seasons: red and yellow leaves in the fall, brown twigs and red berries in the winter, and all the colors of the rainbow in the spring and summer flowers. (See also Activities 39 and 64)

Activity 89   *"What Color, Please, for Parsley and Peas?"*

Distinguishing Colors of Fruits and Vegetables

DIRECTIONS: Next time you and your child are at the market together, spend a little time looking at all the various fruits and vegetables and talking about the different colors. You will be admiring green cabbage, lettuce, and limes; red tomatoes, apples, strawberries, and beets; yellow squash and lemons; orange carrots and oranges; purple grapes and plums; and brown potatoes. If your child has already learned the colors well, you can talk about different shades of color such as light green lettuce and dark green spinach. (See also Activity 64)

Activity 90   *"White Socks, Blue Socks, Red Socks, Too"*

Sorting Laundry
(to learn to organize objects by color groups)

MATERIALS: Laundry to be washed.

DIRECTIONS: Your child will enjoy helping you sort the laundry both before and after it is washed. Before the clothes are washed, you can show him how to make three piles, separating whites, light colors, and dark colors. After they are washed, you can help him sort clothes into separate piles for different members of the family, and talk about the colors as you sort. He might observe, for example, "I have red pajamas and green socks and a yellow shirt in my pile, and you have blue slacks and a brown jacket in your pile." (See also Activities 121, 127, and 141)

Activity 91   "I'm Making a Purple Egg"

Dyeing Eggs
(to show color differences and learn about color combinations)

MATERIALS: Hard-cooked eggs and nontoxic food coloring.

DIRECTIONS: You and your child will first cook and cool the eggs, then dip them in food coloring to make them different colors. You might make a different-colored egg for each member of the family. As you dye and handle the eggs, you should refer to the colors, and your child should tell each family member what color egg she or he is going to get. (Save the eggshells. Your child will enjoy pasting bits of colored eggshells on paper to make pictures or designs.)

Activity 92   "Let's Fish for a Color"

Matching Colors
(to learn to compare and contrast colors)

MATERIALS: Construction paper (different colors), blunt scissors, paste, cardboard, index cards or old playing cards.

DIRECTIONS: Help your child make a set of color cards. Use five different colors and make four cards of each color. Cut the cardboard into "cards" and cover each, on one side only, with a piece of construction paper. When you finish making twenty cards, arrange them so that all of them are face down, and mix up the colors. Let your child turn them over one by one and name the color of each.

VARIATION 1:   Let your child turn over the cards in the pile one by one, as in the activity above. This time, though, he is to look at the card color then lay it face down on the table. He is to call out the color after laying it down, then find some object in the

room that is the same color. If he forgets the color of the card he can go back and look again.

VARIATION 2:   Lay the cards face down and mix them up. Put them in a pile on the table face down. Taking cards off the pile, deal out five cards to each player. The player holds the cards in her hand and puts all the reds together, all the blues together, and so forth. The object of the game is to get a full set of four of any color. The first player asks the player to her left, "Do you have a green?" If the player to the left has a green, she hands it over. If not, she says, "Go fish!" The first player must then draw from the pile on the table instead. If she happens to draw the card she asked for, she gets a second turn. The first player to get a full set of four cards all of one color wins the game.* (See also Activity 95)

---

*From *Learning Through Play* by Jean Marzollo and Janice Lloyd. Copyright © 1972 by Janice Lloyd and Jean Marzollo. Reprinted by permission of Harper & Row, Publishers, Inc., and William Morris Agency, Inc., on behalf of the authors.

IDENTIFYING SHAPES

Being able to recognize different shapes is an important preschool skill, especially for the development of reading and mathematics abilities. Letters of the alphabet are composed of circles, parts of circles, and straight lines. To learn to read, a child must be able to distinguish one shape from another. Numbers are composed of different shapes, too, which must be learned for proper identification. Success with beginning geometric concepts depends on the proper identification of shapes and forms.

Included in this section are several activities that can help reinforce for your child the recognition of shapes. Activity 93 creates an enjoyable situation for a child while asking her to identify particular shapes as she makes them. Activity 94 further emphasizes a creative approach to shapes by having a child cut out her own from potato halves. Activity 95 introduces the game element in identifying shapes, while Activity 96 asks a child to draw the shapes of common household items and correctly identify them.

Activity 93   "I'll Cut a Roof"

Cutting Shapes Out of Bread

MATERIALS: Bread with crusts trimmed, cookie cutters, cookie baking sheet.

DIRECTIONS: If possible, use unsliced bread so you can slice it lengthwise and get more cutting surface. Otherwise, regular sliced bread will serve the purpose. Show your child how to cut shapes out of bread with the cookie cutters (or with a knife, if no cutters are available). The bread cutouts may then be used for making sandwiches or toasted in the oven and used for croutons or bread crumbs.

Activity 94   "One Potato, Two Potato"

Making Prints with Cut Potatoes
(to use shapes to create artistic patterns)

MATERIALS: Raw potatoes (one or two cut in half), tempera (poster paint), paper towel, dish or plastic meat tray, large sheet of paper.

DIRECTIONS: Cut shapes out of raw potatoes, or simply use one cut in half. Spread paper towel in dish or plastic tray. Pour a little paint over it. Show your child how to press the potato down against the towel, then stamp it on the sheet of paper. If you are using several shapes, your child may want to stamp them all on one paper or use a different sheet for each shape.

Activity 95   *"Round Sun and Crescent Moon"*

Making and Using Flash Cards Cut in Shapes
(to help identify different shapes)

MATERIALS: Cardboard, blunt scissors.

DIRECTIONS: Help your child cut out cards with different shapes—for example, squares, rectangles, circles, triangles, crescents, leaf shapes, heart shapes. Pile up the cards on the table. Then you and your child can take turns drawing a card and naming the shape. (See also Activity 92)

Activity 96   *"What Shape Is It?"*

Observing and Naming Shapes

MATERIALS: Objects around the house with distinctive shapes and of a suitable size for tracing; large sheets of paper; pencil, pen, or crayon; blunt scissors.

DIRECTIONS: Collect such things as different-sized plastic jars or glasses, a paper napkin folded into a triangle, a small saucepan, a pie server or pancake turner, measuring spoons. Show your child how to trace around each object and cut out the shape. After he has cut them all out, ask your child if he can match his cut-out shapes to the original objects. As he does this, talk with him about what each shape looks like—for example, a square or a triangle. Finally, your child will enjoy sorting out either the cutouts or the original objects according to shape or other characteristics such as size.

TELLING LEFT FROM RIGHT

Directionality is the ability to know right from left. A child should be aware that there are two sides to the body—the right and the left.

She should be able to use each side separately or both sides together as the task demands. When feeding herself, she learns to use just one hand. When playing the piano, she learns to use both hands at the same time, although each is working independently of the other. As stated in the section on body awareness in Chapter Two—Body Movement, our earliest awareness is of the body as a whole or as a mass. By experimenting with the two sides of the body, we begin to know the left side from the right.

In our culture, it is necessary to develop a left-to-right directional sense in order to learn to read and write. Often parents incorrectly assume a child knows that one begins reading at the left and reads to the right. When reading to your child, point out where to begin. A young child will look at a book or picture from any point of view. She needs to practice moving her eyes from left to right across the page. Not knowing how to do this can cause reading difficulties later on.

Activity 97 reinforces a left-right awareness by providing a physical reminder on one hand of the child. Similarly, Activity 100 emphasizes the difference between left and right by using objects placed in piles on the left or on the right. Activities 98 and 99 use children's songs and dances to reinforce left-right awareness. Activity 101 incorporates directionality as part of a walk with your child. Activities 102 and 103 concentrate on reading and writing readiness.

Activity 97   *"Red Is Right"*

Labeling One Hand or Foot
(to help discriminate right from left)

MATERIALS: A sticker or a piece of tape.

DIRECTIONS: Put a sticker or a piece of tape on your child's right hand or foot, and tell him, "The sticker is on your right hand" (or right foot). For several hours, while he is wearing the sticker, ask him to do certain things with his right or left foot or hand. The sticker will help him to remember which is left and which is right. (See also Activity 2)

Activity 98   *"Left, Right, Left, Right"*

Marching to Music
(to reinforce left-right discrimination)

DIRECTIONS: Sing or play a record of marching music. As you and your child march around the room in time to the music, ask her to call out "Left, right, left, right," as the corresponding foot hits the ground.

VARIATION: "Drum"

Materials: Empty cylinder-shaped box or coffee can with lid; masking tape; yarn or string; spoon; paper and crayons (optional).

Directions: Help your child secure the lid to the box or can with tape. Show her how to tape or tie on some yarn or string so that she can put it around her neck as a drum. Let her use the spoon as a drumstick. If she wants to, she can cover the drum with paper and decorate it by coloring with crayons. Now, as you sing or play the marching music, your child can beat her drum in time to the music and call out "Left, right, left, right," as she goes. (See also Activities 2, 15, and 32)

Activity 99   *"Hokey Pokey"*

Singing and Dancing
(to help distinguish right from left)

DIRECTIONS: Say or sing the "Hokey Pokey" with your child as you both go through the appropriate motions:

Put your right hand in,
Put your right hand out,
Put your right hand in,
And shake it all about.
Do the Hokey Pokey
And turn yourself about.
For that's what it's all about.

You can repeat the above for left hand, right foot, left foot, leg, hip, elbow, and knee, ending with "Put your whole self in. . . ."

VARIATION: Say or sing "Looby Loo." Here are the words:

Now we dance looby, looby, looby,
Now we dance looby, looby, light,
Shake your right hand a little,
And turn you round about.

Now we dance looby, looby, looby,
Now we dance looby, looby, light,
Shake your right hand a little,
Shake your left hand a little,
And turn you round about.

Now we dance looby, looby, looby,
Now we dance looby, looby, light,
Shake your right hand a little,
Shake your left hand a little,
Shake your right foot a little,
And turn you round about.

You can continue adding left and right parts of the body, finally ending with "your whole self," as in the "Hokey Pokey." (See also Activity 2)

Activity 100   *"Knife and Fork"*

Sorting Objects as to Right and Left
(to help learn the uses of "right" and "left" in real-life situations)

MATERIALS: A collection of fairly small household objects or toys for sorting, including a knife and fork.

DIRECTIONS: Pile the collection of objects or toys on a table. Ask your child to put the knife on his right and the fork on his left. Then, as he picks up each object, ask him to put it either in the "left pile" or the "right pile." The familiar left-right positions of fork and knife will help your child remember which is which. You can include in the collection right and left gloves or objects, like a pencil, a crayon, or a spoon that he habitually uses with one particular hand. (See also Activities 118 and 127)

Activity 101 *"Robin on the Right and Dandelions on the Left"*

Identifying Objects on the Right and on the Left

DIRECTIONS: As you and your child are walking or driving along the street, ask her to be your tour guide and call out things of interest on the right and on the left. Some things she might see are dandelions, a dog, a bus, a friend's house, a fire station, and a robin. If you take turns with her as tour guide, she will take great pleasure in correcting you if you joke with her by calling "left" instead of "right."

Activity 102 *"Unroll My Story"*

Emphasizing Left-to-Right Sequence
(to prepare for reading)

MATERIALS: A roll of shelf paper, crayons.

DIRECTIONS: Unroll the shelf paper and lay it flat on a table with the cut edge to the left. Ask your child if he would like to draw a series of pictures to make a story. He should make his first picture at the cut edge and work toward the inside of the roll. When he has finished, roll the paper up again. Your child will enjoy unrolling the paper, telling you the story, and showing you the pictures as he goes along.

Activity 103 *"Chicken Scratch"*

Writing with the Wrong Hand
(to help differentiate between right and left)

MATERIALS: Paper; pencil, pen, or crayon.

DIRECTIONS: Ask your child to write her name or some letters or numbers with the "wrong" hand. She will be surprised and amused at how awkward it feels and how strange her writing

looks. Ask her whether the "wrong" hand is her right hand or her left hand.

LEARNING LETTERS

One of the basic skills of visual perception is the identification of letters of the alphabet. While formal instruction in alphabet recognition and formation does not usually begin until kindergarten, there are many useful activities you can do with your child that will help provide a good foundation. Basic to reading is the quick identification of letters and the ability to associate each letter with a particular sound. Adults take this knowledge for granted, but the process is as foreign to your child as Chinese or Arabic symbols and sounds would seem to most of us.

Activities 104 and 105 ask a child to find letters either in the environment or in a particular medium like a newspaper.

Activities 106, 107, and 110 emphasize the physical design and creation of individual letters by a child. Activities 108 and 109 involve the actual formation of words—Activity 108 by using names of the members of the immediate family and Activity 109 by letting a child choose words to reproduce.

Activity 104   *"Letter Hunt"*

Finding Letters in the Environment
(to increase facility in alphabet recognition)

DIRECTIONS: You and your child can go on a "letter hunt" around the house or around a shopping center. You can take turns suggesting a letter for the other to find, or you can start going through the alphabet and see how far you can get. On a trip, you also can see how many letters you can find on signs, billboards, exit markers, stores, and so on. Another thing you can do is ask your child to find all the letters that spell her name.

VARIATION: You can look for objects that resemble letters. For example, the piece of metal which holds up the chain, on many storm or screen doors is shaped like an S. Cheerios resemble the letter O. A telephone pole looks like a T. (See also Activity 148)

Activity 105   *"I Found a Q"*

Finding Letters in Newspapers and Magazines
(to identify letters on a printed page)

MATERIALS: Newspaper or magazine.

DIRECTIONS: Give your child a magazine or newspaper. You call out a letter, and he tries to find it in the magazine or newspaper. You can call out the letters of the alphabet in order or skip around. As in Activity 104, you can suggest that he find all the letters that spell his name. (See also Activities 143 and 148)

Activity 106   *"Make a New Letter"*

Copying and Learning Letters

MATERIALS: Paper; pencil, pen, or crayon.

DIRECTIONS: Ask your child what new letters she would like to learn to print. When she suggests "M," for example, print the M on her paper and let her practice copying it. If she cannot think of any more letters, suggest some to learn. Your child may enjoy making up a story to go with some of the letters. For example, when she makes a V, she might tell you she is starting at the top of the hill, going down to the bottom, then climbing up another hill. (See also Activity 141)

Activity 107   "Finger Painting, Letter Making"

Making Letters in Finger Paint
(to reinforce the formation of letters)

MATERIALS: Shelf paper, finger paint.

DIRECTIONS: Spread out the paper with the shiny side up. Show your child how to cover the paper with paint. He will enjoy making letters with his fingers and asking you to guess what each one is. You can show him how to make new letters in the finger paint—your letters can be made at the edge of the paper to leave room for him to copy them. You also can call out letters for him to make in the finger paint.
Here is a recipe for finger paint.*

1/2 cup cornstarch
1 quart water
1/4 to 1/2 cup soap
  flakes (not detergent)
vegetable coloring
  (optional)
	Gradually add the water to the starch. Cook over medium heat until mixture looks clear. Add vegetable coloring, if you like. Cool and store, covered, in the refrigerator.

(See also Activities 23 and 142)

Activity 108   "Mrs. J-O-N-E-S Is Grandma"

Learning the Letters in Family Names

MATERIALS: Heavy paper or lightweight cardboard, crayon or pen, blunt scissors.

DIRECTIONS: Cut out enough name cards for all members of the household. Then, either you or your child can print the name

---

*This recipe and others are to be found in Doreen Croft's book, *Recipes for Busy Little Hands,* 585 No. California Avenue, Palo Alto, California 94301.

of each family member on a card. Your child can cut out his own name tag and pass the rest out to family members. You might add symbols to the name cards—flower, tree, kite, boat—a different one for each person.

VARIATION: Cut out small squares of heavy paper, and put one letter of your child's name on each square. Mix them up and let your child arrange the letters in the proper order. You can also do this with the names of other members of the family. You can exhibit any number of letters around the house as your child learns them. Their presence is a good reinforcement.

Activity 109   "Platypus"

Choosing and Learning to Write Interesting Words

MATERIALS: Paper; pencil, pen, or crayon.

DIRECTIONS: Ask your child what word he would like to learn to write. You may be surprised at the words he will choose. Print each word he suggests on his paper and let him copy it several times until he gets it right or wants to try another word. He will take pride in making a collection of words of his own choosing that he can write and read. (See also Activity 69)

Activity 110   "Toothpicks and Raisins"

Using Available Materials to Make Letters

MATERIALS: Toothpicks, raisins.

DIRECTIONS: Show your child how she can make the letters of the alphabet by arranging the toothpicks and the raisins in different ways. When she has made enough letters, she will enjoy eating the raisins.

CHAPTER SIX

Mathematics

Mathematics development is a process of construction, not acquisition (Whitin et al., 1990, p. 6). The focus of attention should always be on the meaning that is being communicated rather than on the form of mathematics itself. Children learn mathematics as part of their social world. Effective math instruction provides children with opportunities to pursue their own interests.

According to Piaget, all learning is an active process, both physically and mentally. Children should be allowed to actively explore and manipulate materials in their environment. By doing so, the child is constructing his or her own knowledge. All children go through an invariant sequence of development, and each child goes through this sequence at his or her own pace. Parents and teachers need to allow children time for spontaneous play and exploration.

Young children should be offered a variety of activities that encourage active problem solving and logical thinking. For example, a child experimenting with a ball of clay may first be aware of the physical properties. Clay can be sticky and smooth. It can be made into shapes. It can be rolled. The parent or teacher may ask, "What can we do with the clay? Squeeze it? Tear it?" The adult, without intruding or interrupting, can respond to the child in a way that encourages the extension of the child's ideas and helps her or him discover that a ball of clay can be made into a flat pancake, and then back into a ball. After much experience in acting on the clay, the child discovers that there is the same amount of clay in the ball as in the pancake.

Many adults approach mathematics with wariness and uneasiness. They are apt to view mathematics not as an exciting "second language," but rather as an alien discipline comprehensible only to mathematicians. Nevertheless, playing with simple mathematical concepts can be both easy and enjoyable for you and your child. In fact, he or she is no doubt doing so already while exploring and playing in his or her environment.

The National Council of Teachers of Mathematics (NCTM) has recommended changes in the teaching of mathematics. They suggest teachers and parents teach mathematics in a way that is relevant, fun, and thought-provoking. According to the NCTM, there are four steps that children should follow so that they can learn to use mathematics effectively to solve problems of all kinds:

1. Derive the mathematics from their own ability.
2. Discover and use the power of abstract thought.

3. Practice.

4. Apply the mathematics to something that is of interest to them (Borose, 1992).

Using the materials and resources in and around your house, you can introduce your child to most of the important mathematical ideas she will need in later life. A young child's perceptions of her immediate surroundings dominate her early thinking. What she sees, hears, touches, tastes, and moves as she plays will become the basis for more sophisticated mathematical processes later on.

Some of the child's earliest mathematical experiences come from observing "sets," or groups of things. Little by little his understanding of the world around him grows as he learns to classify, order, and quantify objects and events. For example, he will discover that fruit in the supermarket comes in many different colors and forms. You will notice that he takes pleasure in sorting out such treasures as dolls, toy cars, and books into separate piles or separate paper bags. This is another reinforcement of the concept of sets. As he manipulates concrete objects, a child is learning three fundamental operations that underlie all mathematical thinking (Williams & Shuard, 1970, p. 17):

> *Classification.* Basic to this operation is the recognition of likenesses and differences among objects. Almost everything we use can be appropriately classified—the difference between balls and blocks, skim milk and whole milk, forks and spoons, cats and dogs. Learning to describe and classify items in one's environment is a fundamental pre-counting skill. A child not only learns what should be grouped together, but he also learns how to count the number of objects in each group.
>
> *Establishing "One-to-One Correspondences."* A child has learned this concept when he realizes that each number refers to a particular quantity of objects in the environment. For example, a child grasps that two dots on a piece of paper can be represented by the numeral 2, or a picture of three horses by the numeral 3. A child gradually learns the idea of one-to-one correspondence by matching one item against another. As he helps set the

table, a child observes that every person in the family gets one fork, one knife, and one spoon. A child may notice that each house gets one newspaper in the morning, or that each visiting playmate gets one cup of water. Also he begins to understand that one object or quantity can be larger or smaller, more or less than another. For example, one family member may get two eggs, while everyone else gets one.

"Seriation" or Establishing a Sequence.   The idea that one item or event follows another is basic in our world of cause and effect, largeness and smallness, or any other comparison which involves quantitative reasoning. Your child can learn to put objects in their proper order or sequence by lining up stuffed animals from largest to smallest, or by arranging rocks in order from heaviest to lightest, or by fitting toy rings of various sizes onto a pole in the proper order.

A child's capacity to use a rich variety of experiences in her immediate environment will help her understand these important mathematical concepts. Her own activities, more than anything else, will bring her to a gradual comprehension of the principles important for later success in mathematics. Practice and reinforcement are vitally important to learning. The active and concrete manipulation of toys, household objects, and other readily available materials is excellent preparation for a child's later ability to carry out similar mathematical operations on a more abstract level.

Four areas that represent fundamental operations basic to mathematical reasoning are (1) describing, classifying, measuring, and other basic processes; (2) counting; (3) awareness of time; and (4) number recognition—an essential tool for other important mathematical operations. Your child's early understanding of these four areas will help set the stage for continuing enjoyment of mathematics and provide a sound footing for later mathematical experience. The activities in the following sections are chosen to include a broad representation of basic concepts within the four areas described above. Use them freely along with ideas of your own.

MATHEMATICAL PROCESSES

Learning to "think mathematically" involves a variety of mental processes. This section works with some of the most important of these: describing, classifying, measuring, ordering, comparing, and others. Observing and describing are basic human processes upon which all thinking and reasoning are based. Simply having your child describe the chief characteristics of various objects is a first step toward helping your child learn to discriminate between like and unlike objects. Learning to distinguish one object from another is as important to mathematical reasoning as it is to the development of spoken language.

The ability to put like objects together helps us reduce the chaos and confusion around us and substitute order, pattern, and structure. Indeed, pattern is the basis of all mathematics.

Looking for patterns trains the mind to search out and discover the similarities that bind seemingly unrelated

information together. This encourages us to see the relationship between the parts and the whole. It develops
a child's ability to see patterns, facilitates the transfer of
knowledge, and the belief that events make sense and
can be logically explained (Baratta-Lorton, 1976).

Once children begin to understand and trust the notion of pattern, they see patterns in other areas such as reading, spelling,
art, and music. If we could not classify the world around us, we
would not be able to function intelligently. We would have to
refer to each flower, carrot, car, animal, or person as a unique
and special entity. Communication would be restricted and cum-
bersome.

Comparing and ordering events or objects is a direct extension of the ability to classify. The idea of one object being larger or
smaller than another, or heavier or lighter, is closely related to
sorting out and classifying the differences between one group of
objects and another. As she ranks individual objects according to
size and shape, a child learns about sets of objects that also can be
rank-ordered. She notices that colors range from light to dark and
that people range from thin to fat or from tall to short.

The ability to measure, first by lining up one object against a
constant such as a length of string or a stick, and then by introducing numbers, leads the child to the discovery that everything
in our world can be compared and contrasted. The idea that one
thing can be the same as something else, or greater, or less, leads
directly to addition and subtraction. Joining two snap beads and
separating them again demonstrates to a child the idea of $1 + 1 =
2$ and $2 - 1 = 1$. The young child does not need any formal math-
ematical terms. The experience to be gained from the mathematical games in this section will be quite enough to provide some
valuable insights.

Finally, activities that deal with patterning are central to concepts such as size, length, shape, volume, distance, and direction.
These ideas will help your child work more effectively with the
above-mentioned processes. Again, direct experience at this point
is more important than theorizing about what it is you are doing.
This section includes sample activities for each of the processes described above.

Activity 111 has your child observing objects and describing
them carefully. Activities 112, 114, 115, 121, and 123 reinforce the

process of classification and begin to explore the idea of comparing and contrasting different objects with each other. Activities 117 and 120 introduce the concept of measurement by illustrating the ideas of direction, area, and length. Activities 116 and 122 extend classification skills by reviewing groups and subgroups. Activities 113, 118, and 119 continue to emphasize the ways people measure quantities of things and arrange them in order.

Activity 111   *"Take a Good Look"*

Describing Objects Carefully

MATERIALS: An interesting object such as a leaf, stone, stick, seashell, caterpillar, snow, sand, animal, or any other object or material your child wants to examine.

DIRECTIONS: Spend some time with your child looking closely first at one object and then at another. Talk over with your child all the interesting features you can think of. Discuss the shape, texture, color, smell, weight, and movement. If you have a magnifying glass, look at the object under the glass. You can take turns and see which of you is the last to think of still one more way of describing an object. This activity is a good way to stimulate your child's curiosity. (See also Activities 59, 66, and 184)

Activity 112   *"Long and Short, Thick and Thin"*

Finding and Comparing Shapes and Sizes
(to begin comparing and contrasting objects
of different sizes and shapes)

MATERIALS: Miscellaneous objects that have distinctive shapes.

DIRECTIONS: With your child, collect objects that have different shapes. They can be pine cones, acorns, balls, rulers, spoons, boxes, weed stalks, sticks of varying lengths, or toys that are square, triangular, rectangular, or round. Talk about the shapes. Pick out obvious differences. For example, place a long, flat stick and a round ball side by side. Your child may enjoy classifying all the objects according to their heaviness, size, color, flatness, or any other characteristics of interest.

Activity 113   *"Whose Foot Is the Biggest?"*

Showing Differences in Length and Width
(to compare sizes, biggest and smallest)

MATERIALS: Large paper bags or heavy brown paper, pen or crayon, blunt scissors.

DIRECTIONS: Open and flatten the bags so they can be used as paper. Spread the paper on the floor. Help your child draw around the foot of each member of the family. For comparison, use only left or only right feet for all the tracings. Show your child how to cut out the foot patterns, and then line them up in order, from smallest to largest. For a more difficult task, see if your child can arrange them all in order of increasing or decreasing width.

VARIATION: Mark the height of each member of the family. Your child can ask each member to lie on a very long strip of paper or to stand against a door or a long stick or pole. Heights can then be compared. This will lead to a discussion about who is taller and who is shorter. (See also Activity 185)

Activity 114   *"Teaspoon, Tablespoon, Cup, and Quart"*

Comparing Kitchen Utensils
(to emphasize relative size, smallest to largest)

MATERIALS: Cups or spoons of several different sizes—measuring spoons or cups are good.

DIRECTIONS: Ask your child to arrange the cups or spoons in order from the smallest to the largest. Start with three or four items and increase the number as your child gains experience putting them in the right order.

VARIATION: You can use drinking straws instead, cut to different lengths. (See also Activity 56)

Activity 115   *"Most and Least"*

Comparing Sets of Objects
(to compare most and least)

MATERIALS: Commonplace items such as a pile of magazines, glasses, hats, spoons, pencils.

DIRECTIONS: Arrange the groups on a table, and see if your child can determine which group has the most objects and which has the least. At first make the differences among the groups obvious, then gradually make them closer to equal in number. After your child selects the most and least, you may want to count with her, to confirm her choice. (See also Activity 118)

Activity 116 *"Now You See Them, Now You Don't"*

Some versus All

MATERIALS: Half a dozen to a dozen similar objects. These could be buttons, Matchbox® cars, crayons, or any collection of objects that are available.

DIRECTIONS: Put the collection of objects on the table. Then, with your child's back turned, take a few objects off the table, and ask your child to look and see whether *all* the objects are still on the table or whether only *some* of them are still there. If at first he has trouble understanding "all" versus "some," you can ask him to take off the table all but a few of the objects, then tell him that *"some* are still there." After he replaces the missing objects, you can tell him that *"all* of them are together again."

Activity 117 *"Let's Make a Path"*

Showing Direction and Area

MATERIALS: A fairly large floor area; a ball of string, a long piece of string, or some other line such as a string of extension cords.

DIRECTIONS: Start your child at a certain point in the room and tell her to stretch the line from where she is to some other point in the room. For example, say, "Carry the line and turn *right* to the chair." Then tell her to carry the line to another part of the room. "Go straight ahead to the fireplace." Continue your directions, using directional terms (left, right, straight, curving, at an angle) until you get your child back to the starting point. Look at the pattern or area you have made. Point out the interesting design she has made—does it look like a circle, a rectangle, or perhaps two triangles? (You may want to plan your directions so that you end up with a preconceived shape.) Your child may enjoy giving you directions so that you can make a shape too. You can then discuss how her shape and yours turned out alike or different. (See also Activity 17)

Activity 118 "The Rice Game"

Measuring and Sorting According to Most and Least

MATERIALS: Rice or dried beans or dried peas, ten plastic jars or drinking glasses of various shapes, rubber bands, spoon or scoop, funnel (optional).

DIRECTIONS: Place a rubber band around each glass or jar, arranging the rubber bands at various heights on the different containers. Ask your child to pour the rice into the jars, stopping at the line marked by the rubber band. After you have filled all the jars up to the rubber bands, help your child arrange them in order, starting with the one having the lowest level of rice and progressing to the one with the highest level. This activity is also good for eye–hand coordination.* (See also Activities 100 and 115)

Activity 119   "Let's Make Cookies"

Measuring and Counting Ingredients
(to use the processes of counting, measuring,
and comparing in real-life situations)

MATERIALS: Utensils and ingredients for making cookies.

DIRECTIONS: The next time you make cookies, let your child help as much as possible. Allowing him to measure, count, mix, and sift reinforces many basic mathematical operations. Ask your child to name the various shapes of the cookies you cut out (triangles, squares, circles, half-moons). Let him count out the number of raisins he needs to make eyes, mouth, or buttons on people-shaped cookies. Does it take more or fewer raisins to make a mouth than an eye? Can he use the same number of raisins for each eye?

---

*Idea adapted from Mary Baratta-Lorton, *Workjobs for Parents*. Menlo Park, California: Addison-Wesley Publishing Co., 1975, p. 23.

Help him count how many cookies he made, and later, how many cookies were eaten and how many were left.*

VARIATION: Let your child make his own "cookies" with clay or play dough. (See also Activity 25)

Activity 120   *"Ruler Tubes"*

Measuring Lengths

MATERIALS: A generous number of cardboard tubes from rolls of paper towels, toilet tissue, or gift wrapping paper.

DIRECTIONS: Cut the tubes to different lengths—some twice as long as the shortest tube and some four times as long as the shortest tube. First show your child how to measure the length of her bed or a couch by laying the tubes end to end like a pipeline. Then repeat the measurement, using the medium-sized tubes, and finally measure with a pipeline of short tubes. For each object your child measures, write down the number of tubes required for each of the three pipelines used. Explain that when you measure with short tubes, you need many more than you do when you measure with long ones. This will help your child grasp the meaning of comparative lengths and distances.

Activity 121   *"One Pile for Big Stones, One Pile for Little Stones"*

Sorting Objects
(to practice using classification skills)

MATERIALS: A number of objects that have at least two characteristics easy to distinguish—for example, curved and round blocks that can also be identified as old or new; black and white buttons that are both large and small; smooth and rough stones that can also be identified as heavy or light.

DIRECTIONS: Ask your child first to sort the objects into two piles, each pile to include one common characteristic. (For ex-

---

*From *Learning Through Play* by Jean Marzollo and Janice Lloyd. Copyright © 1972 by Janice Lloyd and Jean Marzollo. Reprinted by permission of Harper & Row, Publishers, Inc., and William Morris Agency, Inc., on behalf of the authors.

ample, there might be one pile of rough stones and one pile of smooth stones.) Then your child may enjoy sorting the stones again, this time according to size. Ask your child if he can figure out some other ways to group the objects. (See also Activity 90)

Activity 122   *"But I Live in Boston, Not Massachusetts!"*

Subsets
(to show that one set of objects can be a subclass of a larger grouping of objects)

DIRECTIONS: Tell your child that the kitchen, bathroom, and living room are very different, but they are all rooms in the house. Point out that each state has many cities. Explain that when you say "furniture," you could be talking about beds, tables, or chairs. Tell him that when you talk about "my family," you are talking about brothers, sisters, father, mother. Also that "coats" include raincoats, jackets, overcoats, parkas, and windbreakers, and "buildings" can be houses, museums, bus stations, skyscrapers, or stores. If you have kittens, point out that kittens are a special kind (or "subset") of cats—they are baby cats. These ideas and others may not be self-evident to your child, but the concept is important.

Activity 123   *"Making Paper Chains"*

Equalizing, Joining, and Separating
(to show equality, addition, and subtraction)

MATERIALS: A number of strips of paper for making paper chains, paste or glue or a stapler, a wire clothes hanger.

DIRECTIONS: Show your child how to make two rows of paper link chains. Hang them on the clothes hanger. If one is longer than the other, ask your child how to make the two chains equal in length. Show her that you can add links to the shorter one or take links off the longer one to make them equal. Your child may enjoy counting the links to see which chain has the greater number.

COUNTING

The development of counting—the concept of numerousness—comes quite slowly for a young child. Children sometimes learn to recite the names of the first ten or twelve numbers fairly early, but it is by rote, and they fail to use the numbers functionally or in relation to the set of objects being counted.

While rote counting may impress the relatives, it is not mathematics. Until a child can pair or match the number "1" with a corresponding object in a set, "2" with the second item, and so forth, he has not really learned to count.

A child starts his progress toward real counting when he realizes that there is sometimes more than one object of the same kind in his environment. This growth comes from a child's gradual ability to discriminate among items and to recognize their likenesses and differences. At this time, he also begins to grasp the ideas of equal, less than, greater than, smaller, and larger. Thus, the concept of numerousness and the ability to begin comparing and classifying objects are two mutually reinforcing ideas in a child's early mathematical awareness.

The first real breakthrough in counting occurs when a child begins to see a one-to-one correspondence between an object and the symbolic recording of it; for example, ten tokens representing ten trucks. Gradually a child comes to understand that it is convenient to replace the tokens with numbers, spoken or written, and thus to count the trucks without having to use pictures or tokens.

In this section, the assumption is made that your child is beginning to grasp the idea of rational counting—understanding the idea of one-to-one correspondence. Activities 124 and 127 emphasize the physical process of counting objects in the immediate environment. Activity 128 uses the sense of touch to reinforce counting skills. Activities 125 and 129 reinforce the idea of one-to-one correspondence. Activity 132 combines the skill of number recognition with counting. Activities 126, 130, 131, and 133 continue to reinforce the process of counting and one-to-one correspondence.

Activity 124   *"How Many Chairs, How Many Stairs"*

Counting Household Items

DIRECTIONS: With your child, get in the habit of counting things around the house. Either you or your child can write down the totals for the objects your child chooses to count. At various times during the week, you may count the number of chairs, windows, panes of glass within one window, strikes of the clock, doors, dolls, trucks, soup cans, light bulbs, or anything else that appeals to your child.

VARIATION: Your child can draw a picture of each item counted. She can record the total for each item by making the appropriate number of dots under or over each picture.

Activity 125   *"Number Boxes"*

Reinforcing the Correspondence Between Numbers and Objects

MATERIALS: A ten-foot length of shelf paper, crayon or pen, and a collection of small toys or other small objects.

DIRECTIONS: Make a "number line" out of the numerals 1 through 10 (or as high as your child can recognize: 1 through 5, 12, or 20; see illustration). Show your child how to count out the

appropriate number of small objects to place in the empty square above each numeral on the chart.

VARIATION: You can make a number line with numerals in scrambled order, and see if your child can still match the correct number of objects to the numerals on the chart. (See also Activities 129 and 150)

Activity 126   *"Which Is First and Which Is Second?"*

Finding and Counting Hidden Objects
(to reinforce counting in sequence)

MATERIALS: A collection of objects small enough to hide and large enough not to get lost: blocks, toy cars, balls, clothespins, and so on.

DIRECTIONS: Hide the objects around the room so that it is fairly easy for your child to find them. Tell your child to begin the hunt. As he brings you each item, identify it as "the first one," "the second one," and so forth. After your child has found all the objects, count them with him to find out the total number of objects he has found. Your child also will enjoy hiding the objects for you to find. Like you, he should call out "first," "second," and so forth, as you bring him the objects. (Be sure not to include any valuables among the objects in the hunt—your child may really hide them!)

Activity 127   *"A Penny Here, a Marble There"*

Sorting and Counting Sets of Objects

MATERIALS: A box about the size of a shoe box; a quantity of small objects (five to ten of each)—stones, marbles, pennies, corn kernels, buttons, or elbow macaroni—to mix together in the box.

DIRECTIONS: Ask your child to sort the items into separate piles—stones in one, marbles in another, etc. See if she can tell you which group has more objects and which group has fewer, both before and after counting them. At first you should limit the number of items to ten per pile. (See also Activities 90 and 100)

Activity 128   *"Count the Knots"*

Counting by Feel

MATERIALS: A piece of clothesline or rope, a scarf for a blindfold (optional).

DIRECTIONS: Tie a series of single knots in the rope. Ask your child to put on a blindfold (with your help) or simply to close his eyes. Let him count the knots by feeling them. To make things a little more difficult, he can hold the rope behind his back and count the knots by feeling.

Activity 129   *"Cars in Garages"*

Matching Numbers with Objects
(to show one-to-one correspondence)

MATERIALS: Ten empty cardboard milk cartons; ten toy cars or blocks (for make-believe cars) small enough to fit inside the milk cartons; and ten cards numbered 1 through 10, each card to have a different numeral on it as well as the corresponding number of dots.

DIRECTIONS: Cut the milk cartons in half and line them up like garages. Place the numbered cards in sequence in front of the "garages." Ask your child to drive her cars into the garages one by one as you call out the numbers written on the cards. For example, you might say "Number Five Garage," or "Number Eight Garage." If your child can handle this easily, mix up the order of the cards in

front of the garages, or add more garages and more cards with higher numbers. You might also want to try using cards that have either dots or numerals, but not both.* (See also Activities 125, 149, and 150)

Activity 130 "Cootie"

Counting Out the Proper Number

MATERIALS: A pencil, paper, and one die.

DIRECTIONS: The players shake the die and draw a cootie guided by the number of dots that appear on the die. A player must toss a "one" (head) before she is allowed to use those numbers that make the eyes (four), antennae (three), or mouth (five). Likewise, she must throw a "two" (body) before she is permitted to use the number "six" for the legs.

VARIATION: You can use two dice and make a more complicated cootie by adding a nose, more feet, a tail, and so on.

---

*Idea adapted from Mary Baratta-Lorton, *Workjobs for Parents*. Menlo Park, California: Addison-Wesley Publishing Co., 1975, p. 79.

Activity 131   "*Dominoes*"

Counting and Matching Dots

MATERIALS: A box of dominoes.

DIRECTIONS: Spread all the dominoes face up on a table. Divide them into two piles so that each of you has half of them. Start by picking up a domino from your pile and asking, "Can you give me a five?" (to match the "five" end of the chosen domino). If your child doesn't have a five, ask him for the number at the other end of the domino. As soon as you have matched any two ends, put the pair to one side, then let your child take his turn. Encourage him to keep calling out the dot numbers as he plays, and do the same yourself. For example, "I need a three," or "I have a six. Can you give me a six to match?"

VARIATION: Play the actual game of Dominoes with your child, for a more structured activity. Shape and letter dominoes are also available. (See also Activity 141)

Activity 132   "*Stepping Stones*"

Reinforcing Counting, Number Recognition, and Sequence

MATERIALS: Large pieces of cardboard or heavy construction paper, pen or crayon.

DIRECTIONS: Number the "stepping stones" 1 through 10, writing a different numeral on each card. Arrange the cards in numerical order in a pattern on the floor. The stepping stones should be far enough apart so that your child has to jump as she moves from one to another. Tell your child you are going to call out the numbers and she is to jump onto the stepping stone marked with that numeral.

VARIATION 1:   Instead of making a path with numerals in order, you can scatter the stepping stones randomly and call out the numbers in scrambled order.

VARIATION 2:   You can make a second set of stepping stones, marked with dots to match the individual numerals in the first set of stepping stones. Then you can make the game more challenging by mixing the two sets of cards so that your child gets used to counting items in a set as well as recognizing numerals.

VARIATION 3: You can reinforce shape recognition by making your stepping stones in the shape of circles, triangles, squares, and rectangles. Then you can ask your child to jump on "Square Eight" or "Circle Two."

VARIATION 4: A good game for two or more players is called "Twister." You will need ten small cards, each with a different numeral, and a box or hat for drawing. Arrange the stepping stones together on the floor so that all are within easy reach of each other (as in the illustration). Either you or your child starts by drawing a numeral out of the hat. You place your foot on the stepping stone featuring that numeral. With each additional numeral you draw, taking turns, you must touch the new numeral with some part of your body, without losing touch with the previous numerals drawn. Each person who loses her balance or stops touching all the previous stepping stones is out of the game. The game becomes more interesting as you increase the number of players, who get more and more tangled up with each other.

Activity 133   "Hopscotch"

Counting, Jumping in Sequence, and Balancing
(to reinforce number sequence)

MATERIALS: A sidewalk, basement floor, or other large surface; some chalk or tape.

DIRECTIONS: Make a hopscotch court similar to the one illustrated. Start at either "Home" and hop with one foot (or both feet when two boxes are side by side) until you arrive at "Home" at the opposite end of the court. Losing balance or touching the ground where there is no box disqualifies a player for that round. Try it with your child or encourage him and his friends to play. Having "Home" at both ends is easier for young children and also reinforces the reversibility of number sequences. This activity is also good for balance and large-motor coordination. For older children, remove "Home" next to numerals 9 and 10.

VARIATION: Throw a pebble or some other token onto the playing area; when you reach the box where the token is, you must bend over and pick it up. Again, the same rules apply if you lose your balance. Older children may play by kicking the pebble or token from box to box. (See also Activity 11)

TIME CONCEPTS

It is relatively difficult for most children to understand the idea of time, particularly the passage of time, as represented by such terms as "yesterday," "today," "tomorrow," "a week ago," "year," "month," "two hours," and "in the future." By comparison, learning to read the clock is fairly easy. Studying the face of the clock and learning to tell time reinforces the child's skill in numeral identification and sequence. However, "telling time" helps a child with the idea of time only as he connects specific clock positions with daily or weekly events that are important to him. He learns that when the clock hands stand at "eight o'clock," some member of the family will often leave for school or work. When he feels hungry in the afternoon, he is likely to see the clock in its "five o'clock" position. When he feels sleepy, the clock will probably say "eight o'clock" again, a different time from the morning "eight o'clock." (Activity 134 will help your child make connections between clock and events.)

You can help your child grasp the idea of passing time most easily if you start with short periods of time. She can watch the big hand of the clock or use a sand glass or a timer to mark the passage of "three minutes." You can gradually extend the length of time. "In thirty minutes we will be ready to go shopping." "In one week it will be your birthday," "Next month you will be starting kindergarten." Your child can mark off days on the calendar to help her get a sense of the passage of a week or a month.

The idea of relative age often impresses a child at quite an early age. Your child observes how older people, like her grandparents, look and behave, as compared with young people like herself. Even though she may not understand how or why people age, she can grasp the idea that aging is related to the passage of time.

As a child waits for a parent to return from work, he is becoming aware of the fact that it takes time for events to unfold. The same will be true if he watches from day to day as carpenters put up a new house in the neighborhood. Keeping track of his own height and weight from month to month will further reinforce the significance of passing time. (See also Chapter 8, Activity 185)

Do not expect your child to completely understand the concept of time for many years. The idea of "millions of years" is difficult even for adults to grasp. However, these activities will help your child appreciate the importance of time and show her some of the ways of telling and keeping time.

The activities in this section deal with your child's identification of the time of important events (Activity 134), the passage of time (Activities 135, 136, 137, and 139), and the recording of time (Activities 138, 139, and 140).

Activity 134   "What Time Do I Get Up?"

Connecting Time with Events

MATERIALS: Paper plates, paper fasteners, construction paper, pens or crayons.

DIRECTIONS: Help your child cut out several big hands for his clocks and several little hands, using the construction paper. Show him how to fasten these onto the middle of the paper plates with paper fasteners. Write in the twelve numerals. Ask your child what time he gets up, what time he goes to bed, when he goes to his friend's house to play, when he eats, and what time any other important event takes place. By making several clocks, he can leave the hands of each clock in a fixed position and keep it as a reminder of the time of day when a particular event takes place. (This activity also reinforces numeral recognition and sequence.)

VARIATION: On an old sheet spread on the floor or hung on the wall, help your child draw the 12 numerals of the clock. Then show him how to use his body to represent the hands of the clock. For example, straight up and down could be six o'clock—dinner time. (See also Activity 164)

Activity 135 "Timing the Thunderclap"

Listening to the Passage of Time
(to show how sound can measure the passage of time)

DIRECTIONS: The next time you have a thunderstorm, explain to your child that thunder is the noise made by the lightning, but that you hear the noise *after* you *see* the flash. Explain to your child that sound, like everything else, takes time to go from one place to another. If the lightning is close by, you hear the thunder right away. If the lightning is far away, it will take the sound of the thunder several seconds to get to where you are. With your child, you can count the seconds between the lightning and the thunder and figure out how far away the lightning is. Five seconds' delay after the lightning indicates a distance of about one mile.

Activity 136 "How Long Does It Take to Bake a Cake?"

Recording the Passage of Time

MATERIALS: A timing device—a clock, kitchen timer, or hourglass.

DIRECTIONS: Decide with your child what you would like to time. Let your child read the clock or set the timer or hourglass. Observe how many minutes go by while you are accomplishing a particular task such as cooking an egg, baking a cake, toasting a slice of bread, setting the table, or washing the dishes.

Activity 137 "Dad, Are You a Hundred Years Old?"

Making a Timeline
(to show the passage of time)

MATERIALS: A roll of paper or several long pieces of paper to tape together end to end, a pen, and a yardstick (optional).

DIRECTIONS: By hand or with the yardstick, draw a long line on the paper. This is the "timeline." At the beginning of the line, write down some recent past event chosen by your child, an event that involved her. For example, it could be a picnic or a birthday party. Moving along the line, you and your child can keep adding more events in order, as they happen: when your child gets a new puppy, when she takes a trip on a train, when the family moves to a new house, when she cuts her finger.

Another way to make a timeline is to write down a happening for each day. Late in the day, perhaps at bedtime, your child will enjoy deciding what she would like to put down for the day. To create a timeline according to the actual length of time between events, you can mark off the entire line according to days or weeks. Then you can record the first snowfall, for example, then Thanksgiving so many days later, then Christmas or New Year's several weeks after that. You can show your child the difference in the length of the line running from snowfall to Thanksgiving and snowfall to Christmas.

Activity 138   *"Making a Sundial"*

Recording the Sun's Movement
(to reinforce the idea of hours and days)

MATERIALS: A sunny day, a flat surface outdoors (a picnic table or card table), a large piece of white paper about 18 inches

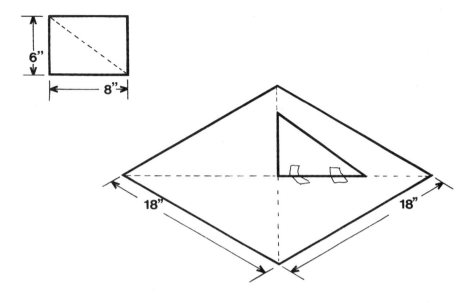

square, a piece of cardboard about 6 inches by 8 inches, tape, and a pencil.

DIRECTIONS: Tape the paper to the flat surface outdoors—be sure it is in a sunny spot. Cut the cardboard diagonally from the top left corner to the bottom right corner. If the cardboard is light-weight, tape the two halves of the cardboard (identical triangles) together, one on top of the other. The cardboard triangle will be your sundial indicator, or "gnomon." Stand the triangle upright so that it will cast a shadow (see illustration).

Tape the 6-inch base of the triangle to the paper on the flat surface. The right angle should be at the center of the paper. The triangle will stand about 8 inches tall. Now let your child mark with a pencil where the shadow falls on the paper. Each hour you can both look at the sundial to see how far the shadow has moved, marking the new location of the shadow each time. Your child does not need to understand the exact mechanics of the sun's movement to appreciate that change is taking place over a period of time. As he marks off the positions of the shadow, he is also learning the value of good observation and recording techniques.

Activity 139   "What Day Is It Today?"

Recording the Days of the Month
(to show recording of passage of time)

MATERIALS: A good-sized current calendar; small nutritious treats (such as nuts or raisins); plastic wrap or waxed paper; and a pen, crayon, or pencil.

DIRECTIONS: Lay the calendar on a table or flat surface. Put one small treat on each day of the month. Each morning your child will delight in picking up the treat for the day. Then you can count with your child to find out how many days of the month have passed already and how many days are left. Your child can cross off each day after she eats her treat. Keep the calendar and treats covered with plastic wrap or waxed paper.

VARIATION: Mark the days of the month on the calendar to indicate when special happenings will occur: birthdays, holidays, a visit by grandparents.

Activity 140   "Spring, Summer, Fall, Winter"

The Seasons of the Year
(to emphasize the passage of time and the
recurrence of cyclical events)

DIRECTIONS: Talk with your child about the seasons. See if he can tell you what season precedes or follows winter or summer. From time to time, ask him what season of the year it is and how he knows. Emphasize the things he can easily observe, such as the migration of birds, colder temperatures, falling leaves, the sprouting of bulbs, and any other telltale signs you can think of. Help him learn the nursery rhyme about the seasons:

> *Spring is showery, flowery, bowery;*
> *Summer is hoppy, croppy, poppy;*
> *Autumn is wheezy, sneezy, freezy;*
> *Winter is slippy, drippy, nippy.*

RECOGNIZING NUMBERS

The objective for "teaching" numbers is the child's construction of the mental structure of number. Learning numbers is very much like the process a child goes through as he begins to realize that letters represent sounds, which in turn make up words and sentences; and words and sentences represent what goes on in the world around him. Math is a language, another way to describe relationships and represent human experience.

As she learns the relationship of numbers to the quantity of marbles in her hand or horse chestnuts in her pocket, the child can take pleasure in the consistency of our use of "1, 2, 3, . . ." Young children begin to understand number concepts when they count. As they count objects, they learn that each object they add represents a higher number. Before children establish this concept, they may count out of sequence or skip objects or numbers. When children recognize that each object is a unit and has a single identity, they can begin to form sets of objects, and soon, combine sets.

Later the child will discover that number concepts by themselves can be manipulated and made to represent other relationships and concepts. At first the insight is intuitive, and only slowly does a child begin to consciously enjoy the fun of using abstract symbols.

This section emphasizes learning number names through active games, as opposed to learning number names by memorization. Thus, the goal here is to focus on the functional and everyday use of number names and concepts so that your child will find them a comfortable and natural part of the world.

Included here are activities that emphasize the recognition of like numbers (Activity 141), number identification (Activities 143, 144, 146, 149, and 151), number formation (Activity 142), and using numbers in real-life situations (Activities 145, 147, 148, and 150).

Activity 141   "Pick Them Out and Match Them Up"

Matching Like Numbers

MATERIALS: A deck of playing cards.

DIRECTIONS: Arrange all the cards in the deck on a table so that the face of every card is showing. Ask your child to find the card numbers that match, and pile all the sevens together, all the aces together, all the fives together, and so forth. If he can manage it, your child will enjoy arranging the completed piles of matched cards in numerical order. (See also Activities 90 and 131)

Activity 142   "Finger Numbers"

Drawing Numbers in Textures

MATERIALS: Waxed paper or a cookie sheet; a substance like sand, salt, or soft clay.

DIRECTIONS: Spread the substance smoothly over the waxed paper or cookie sheet. Let your child practice making numbers in it. To begin with, you might make a numeral, then let your child trace the same path with her finger or make a copy of the numeral next to the one you made. When you want to clear the board for new numerals, just shake it out (salt or sand), or knead it (clay). A fresh surface will be ready for more experimentation. *Note:* You can also make letters and other shapes in the substance. (See also Activity 107)

Activity 143   *"Let's Look in the Newspaper"*

Identifying Numerals in Print
(to learn to identify numerals correctly
and arrange them in proper order)

MATERIALS: An old newspaper, a large sheet of paper, blunt scissors, paste.

DIRECTIONS: Help your child find the numerals 1 through 12 in the newspaper. Let him cut them all out and paste them in order on the sheet of paper. You may have to help him with the sequence if he is not sure. (See also Activities 105 and 106)

Activity 144   *"I Want to Make a Call"*

Identifying Numerals on the Telephone

MATERIALS: A play telephone or a real telephone.

DIRECTIONS: Children love to dial the telephone. If you use a real one, leave the receiver on the hook and give your child one numeral after another to find on the dial in scrambled order: 7, 1, 9, 5. When she finds the correct numeral, she may dial it. Make sure that your child succeeds, even if you have to repeat the same numeral several times.

VARIATION: Let your child dial the entire telephone number when she calls friends or relatives. You can either write it down for her ahead of time or call out the numerals one by one. Watch closely to be sure she dials accurately. (See also Activity 47)

Activity 145   *"My Place Number"*

Using Numerals on Place Mats

MATERIALS: Large pieces of sturdy construction paper or shelf paper; scissors, crayons, or paints.

DIRECTIONS: Help your child cut out place mats from the paper. Either you or your child may write a numeral to be learned in the center of the mat. You can make any number of mats—your child can tell you how many different numerals he wants to learn. He may enjoy assigning "numeral mats" to other members of the family as well as himself. For added reinforcement, you might consider dishing out some foods in servings that match the numerals on the mat. For example, the numeral "4" could indicate four pieces of potato, four chunks of meat, and four carrots. This game should make reluctant eaters more interested in the meal.

Activity 146   *"Which Aisle for Bananas?"*

Reading Numerals at the Supermarket
(to show how numbers are used in everyday situations)

DIRECTIONS: As you and your child shop at the supermarket, make it a point to look at the numerals posted over the aisles. Ask your child which aisle you are in. Then tell her to point out aisle 4 or aisle 6 or whatever aisle is nearby as you move around the store. She will soon be able to tell you the aisle numbers for her favorite foods.

Activity 147   *"What's Our House Number?"*

Identifying Important Household Numerals
(to demonstrate the use of numbers in and around the house)

DIRECTIONS: Go outdoors with your child and write down your house number. Display the numeral prominently inside the house. Write down and display other important numerals such as your child's age and birthdate, or your telephone number or zip code. (You can show him where to find the zip code on incoming mail.) Your child may have a favorite numeral he wants to display. He will enjoy pointing out all the numerals to family members and friends and explaining what they stand for.

Activity 148   *"Number Scavenger Hunt"*

Finding Numbers of Objects around the House
(to equate quantities of objects with number values)

MATERIALS: Twelve cards, each marked with a different numeral from 1 through 12.

DIRECTIONS: Ask your child to select a card with a particular numeral on it and together read the numeral out loud. It might be "3". Then you and your child should see whether you can find three similar objects in the room—for example, three pillows, three chairs, three windows. For a very young child, it might be easier simply to find three unrelated objects—for example, a toy, a sock, and a cup. (See also Activities 104 and 105)

Activity 149   "Cup Toss"

Identifying Numerals
(to reinforce number values)

MATERIALS: Twelve cups numbered 1 through 12 on the underside; a pan to hold the cups (muffin pans work well, but a large baking pan will do if you line it with a towel to prevent the cups from sliding); tokens such as pennies, bottle caps, or buttons.

DIRECTIONS: Show your child how to toss the tokens into the cups. She can try from a distance of about three feet. If this is too difficult, she can stand closer. After tossing a token into a cup, she is to turn the cup upside down and see what the numeral is. You may want to take turns throwing the tokens and seeing what numeral each of you gets. (See also Activity 129)

Activity 150   "Sunny Side Up"

Matching Numerals with Each Other and with Objects
(to reinforce one-to-one correspondence)

MATERIALS: An old egg carton, cards numbered 1 through 12 that will fit inside the sections of the egg carton, and twelve objects such as small blocks or balls numbered 1 through 12 that will fit in the sections.

DIRECTIONS: Place a numbered card in the bottom of each egg carton section. Ask your child to match each block or ball numeral with the same numeral on one of the cards in the egg carton. At first you can arrange the card numerals in sequence in the sections. Later you can make the task more challenging by scrambling the order of the card numerals.

VARIATION: Take the cards out of the carton. Replace them with varying numbers of small tokens such as pennies, buttons, or bottle caps. Instead of cards marked with numerals, you can put eight tokens into one section, five in another, eleven in another, and so forth. Ask your child to count the tokens in a single section. The total might be five. Then ask your child to find the card with the numeral "5" marked on it, and place it in the section with the five tokens. She continues to do the same with each section until all the cards are back in the carton. (See also Activities 125 and 129)

Activity 151   *"I Can Put Humpty Together Again"*
Surprise Picture Puzzle
(to show number sequence)

MATERIALS: An appealing picture cut out of an old magazine, a piece of stiff paper or cardboard to fit the picture, glue or paste, scissors.

DIRECTIONS: Tell your child you are making him a surprise puzzle and that he is not to look until you have it on the table. Paste the picture on paper or cardboard. Cut it into twelve distinct pieces. Turn the picture pieces over and number the pieces from 1 through 12 in such a way that your child will be able to put the puzzle together by following the sequence of the numerals—from top to bottom, or left to right, or any way you like. Keeping the puzzle face down, mix up the pieces and call your child to put the puzzle together. As soon as he has it together, turn it over, and presto—there is a finished picture.

RESOURCES

Baker, A. and J. (1991). *Math's in the mind—A process approach to mental strategies.* Portsmouth, New Hampshire: Heinemann Educational Books, Inc.

Baker, A. and J. (1990). *Mathematics in process.* Portsmouth, New Hampshire: Heinemann Educational Books, Inc.

Baratta-Lorton, M. (1976). *Mathematics their way.* Menlo Park, California: Addison-Wesley Publishing Company.

Bierns, M., & Tank, B. (1988). *A collection of math lessons—from grades 1 through 3.* New Rochelle, New York: Cuisinaire Company of America.

Borose, R. (1992). *Learning mathematics through inquiry.* Portsmouth, New Hampshire: Heinemann Educational Books, Inc.

Lawrence Hall of Science, University of California. (1986). *Family math.* Berkeley, California: Lawrence Hall of Science.

Whitin, D. J., Milles, H., & O'Keefe, T. (1990). *Living and learning mathematics—stories and strategies supporting mathematical literacy.* Portsmouth, New Hampshire: Heinemann Educational Books, Inc.

Williams, E. & Shuard, H. (1970). *Elementary mathematics today.* Menlo Park, California: Addison-Wesley Publishing Co.

CHAPTER SEVEN

Science

Many adults have had negative experiences with science at school. They remember the subject as complicated and full of formulas and jargon. Most of them can give examples of feeling bewildered, lost, and puzzled that the things they were asked to do seemed unrelated to their everyday life. If they carried out practical work, most likely they would have to write about it afterward in a formal way.

It is easy to appreciate the feelings of one child in that position who told his partner, "Don't notice too much. Then you won't have a lot to write." With experiences like this, it is not surprising that people often think of science as a boring, joyless subject that is light years away from the vibrant life of a young child. How wrong they are.

Young children are scientists in their own way. They are born with a scientist's characteristics—they are curious and are continuously exploring and trying to find out about the physical world around them. They view life as their laboratory, observe things, ask questions, test out ideas, and form explanations of events that involve them. Through activities of this kind they develop skills and understandings that help them make sense of the world in which they live.

Adult scientists also do these things, but they do them in much more comprehensive and sophisticated ways. They operate within the rules of the scientific community to which they belong, and their work is systematic and carefully controlled. It frequently requires complicated equipment and is founded on a complex network of abstract ideas that have been built up over time and that shape further progress.

In strong contrast, the miniature scientist works according to her own rules in a trial-and-error manner. Many adults might identify her work as haphazard play. From the point of view of the child, however, this "play" is largely purposeful—she explores and manipulates the things around her. Through this first-hand contact with everyday materials, she builds up her own ideas as to how things relate, how they function, and how she can interact with them. Children and practicing scientists engage in similar processes of discovery. If we wish to help children develop their scientific understanding, we need to sort out some ideas about scientific processes.

OBSERVING

Observation is a key process in science. Young children as observers can never be too active. Your child will need safe opportunities to explore a wide range of materials using all his senses. He needs to see, touch, taste, hear, and smell to get information about objects and events. This information is interesting and valuable in its own right, but it becomes more powerful when it acts as a springboard to other activities such as classifying and sequencing.

When children are observing things, it is fascinating to watch the way they interact with the material. They get messages from it that they reinforce for themselves and frequently wish to communicate with others. Sometimes the communication is through body language. Sometimes it is verbal.

The links between experience and language are so vital that it is important for us to help children build up a vocabulary to describe the observations they make. This does not mean that we should try to force new words into the child's language; that would be counter-productive. Rather, we need to be on the lookout for experiences that could be enriched by new vocabulary. For example, when a child squeezes water from a sponge with obvious pleasure, an adult might helpfully match the activity with words like heavy, light, or "squishy." It is helpful also, as in mathematics, to watch for opportunities to gradually build up the language of quantity (for example, more than, less than) and the language of opposites (for example, rough and smooth).

QUESTIONING

Science is a process of inquiry, and question-raising is a significant feature of all scientific activity. It is also a built-in characteristic of young children, as any parent knows. Sometimes it seems that children never stop asking questions.

Also, some adults may feel inadequate if they do not know the answer to a question. They feel they are failing the child. However, if a child always received an instant "right" answer from an adult, that child's scientific development would be greatly restricted. The reason this is so has to do with the role of questions in scientific inquiry.

Some questions are best answered by concrete action, while others require specific information. Action questions promote science as a way of working. Information questions characterize science as a body of knowledge. Both are important, but it is the action questioning that we most need to encourage in young children. The task is not an easy one, even for practicing teachers, but there are two useful guidelines. First, it may be possible to turn an informational question into an action question. For example, the question might be asked by a child looking in the mirror, "Why am I in there?" The response might be, "Let's see what we can find out. Where else can you see yourself?" In this way valuable experience of the reflective properties of materials can be built up, especially since the original question may be a child's way of just showing interest and not a request for a literal answer.

The second important point concerns the nature of the questions that children hear adults ask—most of them are informational. For example, "Where did I put my pen?" "What time do we leave?" "Are you ready?" Because children catch many mannerisms and styles from adults, it is worth remembering this point. When talking with your child, try to introduce more questions like "I wonder what would happen if _____."

TESTING

Children constantly test their ideas about the way things behave. Watch a toddler pour sand from a container into a tray and then notice the way she does it a second time, and perhaps a third time. We can only guess what is going on in her head, and perhaps guess wrong, but there is much about the action that suggests it is purposeful and prompted by unformed questions. For example, "Will it be the same if I do it again?" "What will happen if I do it differently?" Through such activity children approach the action of experienced scientists. Their ideas and techniques may seem crude and clumsy, if judged by adult standards, but even very young children can predict events on the basis of past experience. They can test materials in light of these predictions and can review happenings for possible reasons.

Unlike mature scientists, children cannot plan ahead in detail. They cannot analyze events with several variables involved, and normally they cannot sustain an inquiry over a significant time span. What they can do and do very well is seek simple solutions to simple problems that arise as a result of their first-hand exploration of materials. For example, a child using a push-along toy on a carpet will often search out other surfaces and repeat the action. The unspoken question is possibly, "Where can I move it more easily?" or "What will it feel like on the kitchen floor?" Both problems are solved by direct action. Later, building on such experience, a child might be challenged to find out which surface is best for pushing a toy along; she can answer through actions. A further possible challenge is to ask if she has used a fair test. Some experienced five-year-olds can cope with the idea of fair testing. ("It wasn't fair because I pushed harder on the concrete.") It's an idea that is slow to develop. However, it is a key concept in science, and lots of exploration involving testing the properties of things will help in its formation.

EXPLAINING

Children formulate ideas to explain the things they observe, but they usually don't share these unless asked. Useful questions, which prompt sharing, are "Why do you think that happens?" "Why do you say that?" "What does it make you think of?" It is vitally important that we accept the ideas children express, even though these may seem very strange. These ideas are the frameworks that help them make sense of the world, and they are likely to be very different from the ideas of adults—especially those of mature scientists.

The five-year-old who says that grapes can be turned into raisins by putting them in water is using the experience of seeing his fingers wrinkle if he stays in a pool too long. Similarly, the seven-year-old who states very firmly that you will find fishbones in gulls' eggs is reasoning from his particular experience of seeing gulls dive into the sea. As the girl who describes the stars as holes in God's carpet is communicating her own ideas, so is the boy who says you can hear sounds from outside a room because they walk through the keyhole.

Children's explanations may seem quaint, but they work for them. They will be adjusted as children gain more experience. What is important is the sharing of these ideas, for this helps children to clarify them. It is also important not to show that you think your child's ideas are strange or for you to try to correct them. With more experience, children's explanations will draw nearer to those of mature scientists.

All the activities that follow can be carried out with everyday materials in familiar situations. Each contributes to the development of your child's scientific ability. Collectively they have been selected to give children experience in scientific skills while helping them develop key scientific concepts.

WHATEVER THE WEATHER

Activity 152   "Windy Days"

Determining Wind Speed

MATERIALS: Two small pieces of fabric about 6 inches square —the same kind, two clothes pins, string, water.

DIRECTIONS: Choose a fairly windy day. Go outside, and together find the windiest place. Then hunt for the least windy place. Look for signs of the wind; for example, leaves moving or branches bending. Can you tell which direction the wind is coming from? Talk about people drying the laundry outdoors. Discuss places that are good for drying clothes and places that are not so good. Choose one of each. Make a clothesline so you can hang up the wet pieces of fabric. Feel each piece every so often. Which place was best for drying? Was it a fair test?

Activity 153   "Sunny Days"

Relating the Sun to Shadows

MATERIALS: Chalk to write on pavement, or large marker pen for writing on a piece of cardboard about 24 by 18 inches.

DIRECTIONS: Choose a sunny morning when shadows are very noticeable. Find a suitable place and draw around your child's feet. Mark the top of her shadow head. Later get her to stand again in the outlines of her feet. Again mark her shadow head. Do this as often as she enjoys it during the day. Talk about the position of the markers. Take this opportunity for shadow play. Can she shake hands with her shadow? Can she hide from it? See if she can notice a pattern in the position of the sun, herself, and her shadow.

(Incidentally, *NEVER* look directly at the sun; it can seriously damage eyes.)

Activity 154 *"Rainy Days"*

Observing the Properties of Water

MATERIALS: Metal jar lid or old metal tray, newspaper, plastic bag. Keep lid and newspaper in the plastic bag until needed.

DIRECTIONS: Choose a suitable rainy day. Go on a rain walk. Look for puddles. How many? Which is the biggest? Can you find hanging drops of water? Any water trickling? How many different rainy day sounds can you hear? Which words best describe them? Put the metal tray on the ground. Watch it get wet. Put the metal jar lid or the metal tray on the ground. What can you see and hear? Will you see and hear the same if you use newspaper? Try it. What will happen with the plastic bag? Talk about similarities and differences in the observations. (See also Activity 182)

Activity 155 *"Count the Cricket Chirps"*

Showing How Crickets Must Respond to Surrounding Temperature While Humans Can Regulate Their Temperature by Such Means as Perspiring or Shivering

DIRECTIONS: If you would like to find out how hot or cold it is outdoors, listen for a chirping cricket in your yard or meadow. Now count the number of chirps in 14 seconds and add 40 to the number you have counted. This number is the temperature. For example, if you count 30 chirps in 14 seconds and you add 40, the temperature is 70 degrees. If the cricket happens to be sitting under a cool, shady leaf, it will give a little lower temperature than where you are standing. If it is in the sun on a warm rock, it will give a little higher temperature than where you are.

Activity 156 *"Put Your Finger on a Cloud"*

Increasing Awareness of Movement of Clouds and Corresponding Wind Speed

DIRECTIONS: With your child, keep your finger very still while you hold it in front of a cloud. Now watch the cloud move past your finger. Sometimes the cloud will go by very fast and sometimes it will hardly move at all. Very little movement means that

the wind speed aloft is low, but if the cloud races past your finger, you know there is a gale blowing up high. Tracking the cloud works best if there is blue sky as a backdrop to the clouds.

Activity 157   *"Find the Wind"*

Introducing Wind Direction and Wind Chill

DIRECTIONS: If you and your child want to find out where the wind is coming from, put one of your fingers in your mouth to make it wet. Take it out and hold it up in the wind. One side of your finger will feel cold which will be where the wind is coming from.

ANIMAL ANTICS

Activity 158   *"Pets"*

Comparing Similarities and Differences of People and Animals

MATERIALS: Your own or your neighbor's pet. (Any safe, four-legged pet is suitable.)

DIRECTIONS: Help your child observe the pet and compare it with his own structure and movement. Look at the eyes. Are they the same color, shape, and position as his? What about the ears? The nose? When the animal is at rest, look for breathing movements. Are they faster or slower than a human being? Compare the pet's fur with human hair. Compare the animal's tracks with human footprints. Watch the pet move from place to place. How many different kinds of movement does the pet have? Can your child imitate some of them?

Activity 159   "Minibeasts"

Observing Different Properties of Animals

MATERIALS: Two fair-sized minibeasts (safe ones) of the same kind; for example, a snail or a worm.* Put them on a large metal lid, and keep their surroundings moist.

DIRECTIONS: Talk about similarities and differences in people. How do people recognize your child and a friend of the same sex? Can we tell two snails (or worms) apart? Encourage close looking. Are there any differences in size? Color? Movement? Markings? Give each minibeast a name. Ask your child to close her eyes; remove one of them. By looking at the minibeast left on the metal lid, can she say the correct name? How did she know?

LIGHT LEARNING

Activity 160   "Looking Through Things"

Understanding Transparency

MATERIALS: Things usually found in the kitchen—bottles, glasses, canning jars, plastic bags, clear plastic containers.

DIRECTIONS: Have an "I can see through it" hunt. You might start by laying a clear plastic bag on a newspaper photo and showing your child, "Look, I can see the picture through the bag. I wonder what else we can see through." Make a collection of see-through things. Sort them into two groups—"easy to see through,"

---

*If you cannot find a snail or worm, use two leaves from the same tree or two flowers from the same plant.

and "not so easy to see through." Which is the easiest to see through? Which is the hardest to see through? You might like to use the word "transparent" to describe see-through things. When you are outside, look for transparent things.

Activity 161   "Looking in Things"
Studying Reflection

MATERIALS: Reflecting things usually found at home—mirrors, shiny metal objects including spoons, an enlarging mirror for shaving or make-up.

DIRECTIONS: Have an "I can see myself" hunt. You might start after your child has been using a mirror. Where else can he see himself? Most likely he will search out all the mirrors. Help him extend his experience by sharing your experience. "Look, I can see myself in the picture glass, and the steam iron, and the toaster." This will help him search out similar objects. Encourage him to observe curved reflecting surfaces such as the front and back of a spoon, or curved mirrors. Help him try to classify his experience. For example, "I see myself clearly/not clearly," "I see myself right side up/wrong side up," or "I see myself the same size" or "I see myself smaller/larger." When you and your child are outdoors, look for reflecting things such as puddles, ponds, plate glass doors, automobile bumpers.

Activity 162   "Mirror Play"
Showing the Reflective Properties of Light

MATERIALS: Two small mirrors (preferably plastic, for safety); flashlight (powerful, but not so strong that it will hurt your child's eyes if he looks directly at it); dark vertical surface, for example, a blackboard.

DIRECTIONS: Get your child to stand about two feet from the dark surface holding a mirror that faces the surface. Now position the flashlight so that light is reflected from the mirror onto the surface. What happens if the flashlight stays in the same position but the mirror is moved? Vary the position of the flashlight. Can your child "catch" its light to make a reflection on the surface? Can she "catch" and aim the light to "hit" particular objects or parts of

objects? Arrange the flashlight in a suitable position and use the second mirror to play a game chasing each others' spots.

SOUND SENSE

Activity 163   "Drumming Sounds"
Comparing the Relative Pitches of Drums

MATERIALS: Some "drums" from the kitchen; for example, a metal roasting pan, cake tin, plastic bowl, wooden spoon, metal spoon.

DIRECTIONS: Place the cake tin upside down. Ask your child to bang the drum with the wooden spoon. Does she like the sound? Get her to touch her fingers gently on the cake tin and bang again. Can she feel a tingle? Try using the other drums. Do they make a higher or lower sound? Do they tingle less or more? Encourage your child to arrange the drums in a sounding order. Will the order be the same if the drums are hit with a metal spoon?

Activity 164 *"Ticktock Goes the Clock"*
Teaching Sound

MATERIALS: Small clock with loud tick, carton large enough to contain the clock, towel large enough to go around the carton, a quiet place.

DIRECTIONS: Listen to the sound of the clock. Copy its sound with your voice. Encourage your child to listen to the sound with the clock held against one ear, the other ear, and his forehead. Now put the clock on a flat surface. Ask him to walk slowly away from the clock and stop when he no longer hears its tick. Put the clock in the carton. How far away now? Show him the towel, and tell him you are going to use it to wrap up the carton and the clock. Ask him to stand where he thinks he will stop hearing the clock. Try it. Did he make a good prediction? Talk about loud noises and how ear plugs protect ears.

WATER PLAY

Activity 165 *"Floating and Sinking"*
Demonstrating the Density of Objects

MATERIALS: Dishpan full of water; several common objects such as an apple, a potato, a coin, a cork, a pasta shell.

DIRECTIONS: Play a game with your child. Show the coin. Ask what will happen if we put it in water. Try it. Point out that it sinks. Now show the cork. Ask if it will sink. Try it. Point out that it floats. Now try each of the other objects in turn. What will they do? Let her try. Then help her sort the collection into floaters and sinkers. Can she make a floater sink? Can she make a sinker float?

Activity 166 *"Making Boats"*
Determining What Will Sink or Float

MATERIALS: Pieces of foil about 6 inches by 6 inches, dishpan of water, packet of marbles.

DIRECTIONS: Play "Let's make a boat." Give your child a piece of foil and take one yourself. Let him take the lead. Most children

will make a boat shape no matter how unsophisticated. Make yours like his, only slightly smaller. Will the boats float? Try it. Will they carry cargo? Try adding marbles until each boat sinks. Which boat had the most cargo? Can you make a boat that floats, carries cargo, and moves quickly through the water when you blow on it?

Activity 167 *"Squirting Fun"*

Tracing the Trajectory of Streams of Water

MATERIALS: Two small plastic containers that had contained liquid soap—they should be flexible enough for your child to squeeze with both hands; a bucket of water outdoors; chalk.

DIRECTIONS: Let your child play freely with the containers in water. Most likely she will learn to fill them with water. If not, show her how. Play squirting games. Mark a circle on a wall or fence about as high as your child's shoulder. Get your child to stand about two feet from the mark. Can she squeeze a container so that a stream of water hits the mark? Which container squirts the best? Squeeze a container so that your child can see the shape of the water jet. Can she trace the shape in the air? Will the shape be the same if she changes the angle at which she holds the container? Have fun squirting different shaped jets into the bucket.

Activity 168   "Pushing Water"

Showing Displacement of Liquids

MATERIALS: Glass bowl or large drinking glass, smaller drinking glass that fits inside the larger one.

DIRECTIONS: With your child, fill the bowl or large glass half full of water. Use the smaller glass like a plunger to push the water down. When you do that you will see the water level go up in the big glass. When you lift out the smaller glass you will see the water level in the big glass go down again.

MOVING THINGS

Activity 169   "Round and Round"

Comparing and Contrasting the Properties of Wheels

MATERIALS: No special materials, but an old baby buggy wheel would be useful.

DIRECTIONS: When you are outdoors, play an "I spy wheels" game. Perhaps you could record what you find in a little book.

- Look for things with one wheel, two wheels, three wheels, four wheels, more than four wheels. Which is most common? Which is least common?
- Look for things of the same kind, like trucks, that have different numbers of wheels. Do the biggest trucks have the most wheels?
- Look for big wheels and little wheels. What are the biggest and smallest wheels you can find?
- Look for wide wheels and narrow wheels. What are the widest and narrowest wheels you can find?
- Look for things with wheels inside.

If you have an old wheel, encourage your child to explore its movement on different surfaces. Which surface lets the wheel move most easily?

Activity 170   *"Let's Take the Elevator"*

Experiencing Up and Down

MATERIALS: Small toy car, three bricks or books, firm plank about 3 feet long and 8 inches wide.

DIRECTIONS: Make a ramp by supporting one end of the plank on a brick. Set the toy car down at the top of the ramp. Let go and watch the car. How far does it travel? Now make the slope steeper by using two bricks. Ask your child how far the toy car will travel now. Try three bricks. Talk about up and down slopes. Which are easier when you are walking on them? When you are outside around the neighborhood, look for structures that make moving up and down easier. How many of the following are in your neighborhood: steps, ramps, elevators, escalators, cranes? Encourage your child to make drawings or paintings of some of these.

SHOPPING EXPEDITION

Activity 171   *"Food Forms"*

Examining Varieties of Food

MATERIALS: Things to be seen in a supermarket.

DIRECTIONS: Introduce your child to the different forms of food available. Locate fresh, dried, frozen, and canned food. Reinforce observations by using structured sentences to describe different types of food; for example, "This apple is fresh." "These raisins are dried." Show your child that the same food may come in several different forms; for example, "These grapes are fresh. When they are dried, they are called raisins. These plums are fresh. When they are dried, they are called prunes."

Activity 172   "Many Wraps"
Showing the Different Kinds of Protective Packaging

MATERIALS: A shopping load.

DIRECTIONS: When you unpack your grocery shopping load, encourage your child to observe different kinds of packaging. It is helpful to build up the idea that the packaging protects the contents in some way, or makes it easier to serve the food. Try using structured sentences to describe the various kinds of packaging— "This package keeps the cookies from breaking." "This special carton prevents the eggs from getting smashed." After your child has had experience with a wide variety of packaging materials, try pointing to new examples and ask, "What does this do?" Experiences like these help build ideas about the relationship between the properties of materials and their uses.

MANY MATERIALS

Activity 173   "Different Materials"
Distinguishing Metal, Wood, and Plastic Objects

MATERIALS: Cupboard or drawer containing metal, wooden, and plastic objects; the words "metal," "wood," and "plastic" printed as labels.

DIRECTIONS: Have your child beside you when you open a cupboard or a drawer. Take out a wooden object. Tell her what you use it for. Let her handle it. Put it beside the label "wood." Invite her to find another object made of wood to join the first. Do the same with a metal object and then a plastic one. Are there any objects in the cupboard or drawer made of metal and wood, metal and plastic, or plastic and wood? Can she find those things that have no metal, wood, or plastic? Are there metal, wood, and plastic things in all the rooms? Which is the biggest wood object? Which is the smallest? How about the biggest and smallest metal object? Plastic object?

Activity 174   "Sorting Games"
Comparing Properties of Objects

MATERIALS: Two lengths of tape or rope about 5 feet long; box of various objects that consist of a wide range of properties—for example, hard/soft, rough/smooth, stretchy/not stretchy, bendy/not bendy.

DIRECTIONS: Arrange the ropes or tapes on the floor in two circles side by side. Invite your child to play a sorting game. Take a soft object out of the box. Say it is soft; let him feel it. Put it in one of the circles. Now select a hard object. Say it is hard, let him check, then put it in the other circle. Can he choose another soft object and put it next to the first in the soft circle? Clear the circles, repeating "soft" or "hard" as the objects go back in the box. Repeat the game using other properties.

PLANT TIME

Activity 175   "Growing Seeds"
Observing the Germination of Plants

MATERIALS: Paper towels; shallow containers such as saucers; a few ounces of seeds for sprouting such as alfalfa, clover, or radish.

DIRECTIONS: Pour the seeds onto a paper towel. Talk about them—their color, size, and shape—and how tiny they are. Can your child pick one up? This is a difficult task for small fingers. Ask her what she thinks it will look like if it grows into a plant. Would she like to help you grow some? First fold the towel in two. Put it on a saucer and dampen it. Now sprinkle about one third of the seeds on the paper towel and put the saucer in a warm, light place. Involve your child in sowing two more sets of seeds, one of them in a dark cupboard. Invite your child to choose another place for the third set. Check every day to be sure the paper is damp, but not

soaking wet. Which seeds germinate first? How different are the three sets?

Activity 176   "Flower Forms"

Examining the Properties of Flowers

MATERIALS: Two good-sized colorful flowers, different from each other.

DIRECTIONS: Talk with your child about the flowers. Which does he like best? Most likely he will base his views on smell or color. Encourage looking closer. Can he make the shape of the flower with his hands? What would it be like if he were small enough to walk around inside the flower? How many different parts would he visit? Do any of them smell? Are any of them powdery? Are any of them sticky? When you are out in the neighborhood, look for other flowers of similar shapes and other flowers of different shapes. Do any of them have insect visitors? Which of them smells? Which smell do you like best? Which smell is strongest?

CURIOUS COOK

Activity 177   *"Cooking Changes"*
Demonstrating Bigger-Smaller, Harder-Softer

MATERIALS: Cooking ingredients.

DIRECTIONS: When you are cooking, encourage your child to notice changes of sizes and structure after cooking. Make a simple chart to record observations. For example, good headings are:

> These get bigger—cakes and rice
>
> These get smaller—meat and mushrooms
>
> These get harder—biscuits, toast, and jello
>
> These get softer—rice and pasta

Activity 178   *"Change and Change Again"*
Illustrating the Three Properties of Water

MATERIALS: Two ice cubes, two deep saucers, two small plastic bags that can be closed tightly.

DIRECTIONS: Let's have fun with ice cubes. Put each ice cube on a saucer. Encourage your child to observe them closely. Can she tell them apart? Talk about differences and similarities. Invite her to choose a place where she thinks one cube will melt quickly and a second place where the other cube will melt slowly. Look at the cubes every few minutes. How are they changing? When both have melted, pour the water from each into separate plastic bags, and close them tightly. Put the bags in the freezer. When they are frozen, put each on a saucer after you take them out of their bags. Are they the same as the original cubes? Encourage talk about the sequence of events. The ice melted and changed to water. The water froze and changed to ice. Keep a lookout for other things, like chocolate, that change when they get warm and change again when they get cold.

Activity 179   *"Where Did the Water Go?"*
Illustrating the Three Different Forms Water Can Take

MATERIALS: Ice cube or icicle, small saucepan.

DIRECTIONS: Put the ice in the pan on low heat—just warm enough to melt it. Watch the ice get smaller and smaller until there is only water in the pan. Now heat the water in the pan to the boiling point. You will then see steam rising from the pan, demonstrating how water takes three different forms.

Activity 180   *"Spin the Egg"*

Demonstrating the Difference Between the Behavior of Liquids and Solids Inside the Egg

MATERIALS: Three eggs with no cracks in the shells, small saucepan, salt.

DIRECTIONS: Leave one of the eggs raw. Soft boil the second egg (about three minutes). Hard boil the third egg (about twenty minutes). Use salted water to prevent the eggs from cracking. Let your child try spinning the raw egg, using both hands. The egg will spin very slowly and it will wobble. Next, spin the soft-boiled egg. It will spin a little faster than the raw egg. Finally, spin the hard-boiled egg vigorously for your child. You will find that it will stand on end and will not wobble. If someone gives you an egg and you don't know whether it is hard or soft, this is the way you can find out.

PARTY TIME

Activity 181   *"Wrap It Up"*

Testing the Properties of Wrapping Paper

MATERIALS: Two fairly small boxes, tissue paper large enough to wrap one box, another kind of wrapping paper for the other box (use regular gift paper or metallic), scotch tape.

DIRECTIONS: Choose a time when wrapping presents has some significance for your child. Suggest he might like to wrap up something. Give him one of the boxes and the tissue paper. Help him wrap the package. It is a difficult task for small hands so don't expect too neat a job. Then ask if the tissue paper was good for wrapping. Would the other kind be better? Talk about the properties of wrapping paper that are important. Does it tear easily? Is it easy to fold? Is it easy to write on? Perhaps your child can invent

a test to find out which wrapping paper is the strongest. He might tear the paper a little or pull on it. Praise any suggestions he may have.

Activity 182 *"Make a Rainbow"*

Observing Colors Float Through Water

MATERIALS: One gallon glass jar, food coloring, water.

DIRECTIONS: Fill the glass jar with water. It is best if the water sits briefly so that the currents from the top can subside. Place one drop of the primary colors (red, yellow, blue) in the jar. Observe the colors as they slowly spread through the water forming patterns and shapes as they blend into colors of the rainbow. To expand on this activity, use a variety of colors to blend new colors. Try hot water; drop the colors in from different heights. Discuss diffusion. (See also Activity 154)

Activity 183   "Is It Magic?"

Observing a Chemical Reaction

MATERIALS: One glass jar or pitcher, three teaspoons of vinegar, two teaspoons of baking soda, vegetable dye, mothballs.

DIRECTIONS: Fill the jar or pitcher with water, then slowly stir in the vinegar and the baking soda. Add a couple of drops of vegetable dye and drop in a few mothballs. The mothballs will sink to the bottom at first, but then they will start to rise to the top. (This experiment works because vinegar is an acid and baking soda is a base. When combined it causes a chemical reaction that produces carbon dioxide bubbles.)

USING OUR SENSES

Activity 184   "What Did You See?"

Observing and Appreciating the World Through Our Senses

DIRECTIONS: Observing the world and being receptive to what lies around you and your child is an excellent opportunity to experience and feel the sense of wonder about life. It also helps support her intellectual curiosity, independence of mind, and faith in reason. The following are some activities that can use the senses:

1. Get a magnifying glass and look at objects you take for granted as ordinary or uninteresting; for example, sand grains, flower petals or leaves, snow, or an insect.
2. Gaze at the stars on a clear night and try to get lost in them. Observe the constellations, the twinkling of the stars, the elemental and grand loneliness of the whole sky.
3. Take a flashlight out at night and see what you can find in the grass, garden, or flowers. See if you can find the cricket chirping or any other little creature that is making some noise.
4. Feel and compare various items like clothes, food, trees, or anything else that looks interesting to touch.

5. See what you can smell when you take a walk; for example, wood smoke, the smell of the ocean, the woods after a fresh rain.

6. Take time to listen to the sounds of nature: thunder, the wind, running water. Sometime, when both you and your child are up, go out at daybreak and listen to the rising chorus of birds as the sun rises. (See also Activity 111)

CHAPTER EIGHT

Social and Emotional Development

We are all social beings. We cannot function effectively as humans unless we have satisfying relationships in our lives. Interaction with others gives us our "humanness." Our adjustment and fulfillment depend on the feedback we receive from those around us who are important in our lives.

The communication channels between child and adult are in a continuously delicate balance. One affects the other during every minute of interaction. A child's happiness just as surely influences an adult's good feelings as an adult's emotional state affects a child. However, the daily ups and downs in human relationships are not as influential as the long-term, prevailing moods and messages, both verbal and nonverbal, that are conveyed to a person.

Children can survive passing crises such as a parent's anger at a child for breaking a glass. A person's feelings about himself or herself are determined by the long-term messages sent by others including: degree of acceptance, caring attitude, belief in the other's capabilities, openness in the relationship.

Psychologists have spent much time describing the characteristics of a good relationship: honesty, warmth, the ability to listen and empathize, the capacity for supportive behavior. This chapter includes three areas which reinforce traits that are vital to good relationships:

1. *Self-concept*—The concept of self is the foundation on which social and emotional stability rests. People gain their self-concept from the way important people in their lives treat them. Closely intertwined with self-concept is the next area—a child's ability to interact with others.

2. *Relationships with Others*—It is essential that a child find enjoyment in social relationships and develop skills in relating effectively to those around him or her.

3. *Assuming Responsibility*—A child must learn to become a productive and functioning member of society, whether this is the family, a classroom, a church group, or some other social unit.

The activities in this chapter are intended to help support an acceptance of children and respect for them as individuals striving to be fully functioning, independent beings. Immature behavior on the part of a child is usually an honest attempt to resolve the tensions arising from the complexities of the world. Many of the

activities help to give the child confidence that other people will listen to what he has to say and will value his words and deeds. A child will be motivated to act more responsibly if he feels that what he says and does will be respected and taken seriously by those people who are most important to him.

SELF-CONCEPT

The self-concept of an individual includes the sum total of perceptions, attitudes, and beliefs about herself which she considers to define "me." Her experiences keep modifying her self-concept, but some deeply held beliefs she has stay relatively constant. When we talk of a poor or good self-concept, we are referring to what a person generally thinks about herself, both privately and in social situations. Depending on the feedback she receives from people around her, a person may perceive herself as a good student, an average baseball player, a loyal friend, a timid person, a sensitive artist.

This section emphasizes the simple, direct ideas that give your child a happy, secure feeling and a sense of identity. Activities 185,

190, 191, and 192 help define the unique characteristics of your child and highlight the kinds of life events that make strong impressions on a child. Activities 188 and 189 stress awareness of moods and feelings. Activities 186 and 187 reinforce a child's identity as an important person whom others recognize as such. Activity 193 contributes to a sense of self and to an awareness of a child's place within her or his family.

Activity 185   "How Big Am I?"

Measuring Your Child
(to help your child feel proud of growing and changing)

MATERIALS: A yardstick (or a permanent measurement chart you can attach to the wall), paper, tape.

DIRECTIONS: Tape some pieces of paper to a blank wall (or use a premeasured chart) and record your child's height each month. You can discuss his growth and what it means to reach certain heights. For example, at some community pools, children can begin swimming lessons as soon as they are as tall as the shallowest part of the pool. Emphasize the steady progress your child is making. If you want to, you can also keep a separate chart of your child's weight, recording it once every month and telling him how much he has gained. *Note:* Recording height and weight is also good practice for your child in learning how to measure. (See also Activity 113)

Activity 186   "Any Mail for Me?"

Receiving Mail

DIRECTIONS: Enroll your child in a book club or order a magazine subscription for her (see below for sources). Put it in her name. There are several children's book clubs that will send books periodically to your child at a reasonable cost. It's a thrill for a child to receive mail with her name on it. Receiving books is also a good way to build your child's personal library.

Magazines Published for Young Children (generally for ages two or three to six or seven):

1. *Humpty Dumpty's Magazine.* Children's Better Health Institute, Benjamin Franklin Literary and Medical Society, Inc.,

1100 Waterway Blvd., P.O. Box 567, Indianapolis, IN 46206. Supposedly a health, nutrition, and safety magazine, the publication seems to have more of a general interest focus.

2. *Sesame Street.* Children's Television Workshop, One Lincoln Plaza, New York, NY 10023.   Similar in format to the television show.

3. *Highlights for Children.* 2300 W. Fifth Ave., P.O. Box 269, Columbus, OH 43272-0002.

4. *Chickadee.* Young Naturalist Foundation, 56 The Esplanade, Toronto, Ontario M5E1A7 Canada.   Contains items that will interest children in their environment and in the world around them.

5. *Ladybug.* Carus Corp., 315 Fifth St., Peru, IL 61354.   Contains numerous learning activities with a particular focus on reading and understanding.

6. *Lollipops.* Good Apple, Inc., 1204 Buchana, Carthage, IL 62321.   Good stories, puzzles, riddles.

7. *Snoopy.* Welsh Publishing Group, Inc., 300 Madison Ave., New York, NY 10017.   Composed of articles, stories, mazes, matching puzzles, recipes, and posters starring the famous Peanuts Gang.

Book Clubs for Young Children (specify the age of your child when you write or call for information)

1. Books of My Very Own. Book-of-the-Month Club, Inc., Time-Life Bldg., Avenue of the Americas, New York, NY 10020; tcl: 212-522-4200.   Hardcover and softcover books, new titles and classics for four reading groups, from babies to ten-year-old readers.

2. Children's Book-of-the-Month Club. Book-of-the-Month Club, Subsidiary of Time Warner Inc., Time-Life Bldg., 1271 Avenue of the Americas, New York, NY 10020; tel: 212-522-4200.   A book club that highlights one selection a month for four age groups, from babies to age twelve and provides 50 titles to choose from.

3. Children's Choice. Newbridge Communications Inc., Subsidiary of K–III Holdings, 333 E. 38 St., New York, NY 10016; tel: 212-455-5000.   Classic and award-winning hardcover books from major publishers for children ages 2 to 7.

4. Early Start. Newbridge Communications, Inc., Subsidiary of K–III Holdings, 333 E. 38 St., New York, NY 10016; tel: 212-455-5000.   Classic storybooks and board books for children age 6 months to 2 years.

5. Firefly Book Club. Scholastic Inc., 730 Broadway, New York, NY 10003; tel: 212-505-3000.   Preschool book club, offering hardcover and softcover books on all subjects for children age 0 to 5 years.

6. Junior Library Guild. 1540 Broadway, New York, NY 10036; tel: 212-782-8943.   Hardcover selections from children's book publishers; seven age groups, preschool through high school.

7. Parents Magazine's Read Aloud Book Club. Division of Gruner and Jahr USA Publishing, 685 Third Ave., New York, NY 10017; tel: 212-878-8700.   Original hardcover picture books from *Parents Magazine* Press for boys and girls ages 2 to 7.

8. Troll Book Clubs Inc. 100 Corporate Dr., Mahway, NJ 07430; tel: 201-529-4000 or 800-526-5289.   Grades pre-K to 12.

9. Trumpet Club. Subsidiary of Bantam Doubleday Dell, 1540 Broadway, New York, NY 10036; tel: 212-354-6500.   Ages Pre-K to 8. (See also Activity 63)

Activity 187   "My Letter, Your Letter"

Sending and Receiving Mail
(to teach your child the joy of exchanging
written communications)

DIRECTIONS: You and your child can make a letter or picture-letter for each other. Put them in separate envelopes addressed to each other, stick on a stamp, and take them to the mailbox. The two of you can then wait for the mailman to bring them a day or two later. You can also have your child mail the letter to anyone who will write back—siblings, friends, grandparents, uncles, or aunts. Your child can dictate the message to you.

Activity 188   "All My Faces"

Making Pictures of Your Child's Moods
(to help recognize and understand feelings)

MATERIALS: Paper, crayons, or paints.

DIRECTIONS: Have your child draw a picture of himself as he might look when he is feeling various emotions. He could draw several selves; for example, one happy, one sad, one angry, one scared. (He might enjoy looking in a mirror to check out various faces before drawing them.) Talk about the pictures with him. When he is finished, put up his pictures on a wall (without labeling them.) Ask him to point to the picture that shows the way he feels. Later, when your child gets into a particular mood, you can take him over to the appropriate picture and ask him if that is how he feels. This can help your child recognize his feelings and understand that his moods keep changing. Your child may also enjoy making pictures of parents in different moods.

VARIATION: Instead of drawing pictures, make masks from paper bags to show different feelings. Your child will enjoy acting the part for the different moods as he changes masks.

Activity 189   "I Feel Happy, I Feel Sad"

Using Open-Ended Sentences to Discuss Feelings
(to help your child express why she feels the way she does)

DIRECTIONS: Play the following game with her (either one of you can begin). Complete each sentence.

I feel happy when _____

I feel sad when _____

I feel afraid when _____

I feel excited when _____

I want to go to my room when _____

I want to be by myself when _____

This game is an excellent way of teaching your child to recognize and stay in tune with her emotions and yours. Dealing with these openly and honestly is a way of gaining self-control and emotional maturity.

VARIATION: When something especially pleases you or your child, or something is bothering either of you, you can use what are known as "I-Statements." For example, you might say to your child, "I am happy when you pick up your toys after playing with them," or "I am sad when you forget to feed the cat."

"When you _____ , I feel _____ because _____ " is another version of an "I-Statement."

Activity 190   *"Today"*

Keeping a Diary
(to orient your child to important past, present, and future life events)

MATERIALS: Blank notebook or sheets of paper fastened together, pen or pencil, old magazines to cut out, blunt scissors (last two items optional).

DIRECTIONS: Help your child keep a diary. Set aside some time after a trip, a visit from grandparents, a birthday party, or a special project to write down what happened. Enter the time, place, and date at the top of a piece of paper and then ask your child:

1. "What shall we say about what happened?"
2. "What do you remember about it?"
3. "What things did you like the most?"

Write down whatever your child dictates. Your child might also paste or tape souvenirs or other reminders of the trip or special event into the diary. Let your child include anything he wants— pebbles, drawings, seashells, birthday cards (it will probably get pretty bulky!). He can also give you suggestions for titles or stories about the various items that you can write down.* *Note:* This activity is a very good reading and writing exercise. (See also Activities 71 and 137)

Activity 191   *"How Am I Special?"*

Listing Personal Characteristics
(to make your child more aware of personal uniqueness)

DIRECTIONS: Discuss with your child all the things that make her a unique individual. At first you might want to give suggestions. Start with fairly common things that give your child

---

*From *Learning Through Play* by Jean Marzollo and Janice Lloyd. Copyright © 1972 by Janice Lloyd and Jean Marzollo. Reprinted by permission of Harper & Row, Publishers, Inc., and William Morris Agency, Inc., on behalf of the authors.

her special characteristics. It could be brown or blue eyes, black or blonde or red hair, long eyelashes, freckles, her height, a special pet she owns, or anything else that will make your child feel a special pride about her particular attributes or possessions. Then you can play a simple game called "What is special about me?" Each of you takes turns listing things about yourself and the other that you consider special. When both lists are finished, you can read them aloud. A closely related game is "What do I like about myself?"

Activity 192   "Book about Me"

Making a Booklet about Your Child
(to help recognize uniqueness as a person)

MATERIALS: Some sheets of paper you can bind, staple, or tie together; crayons or paints; scissors; old magazines to cut up.

DIRECTIONS: You can make certain suggestions, but, as much as possible, let your child choose which pictures to make or cut out and where to place them in his book. He will enjoy pictures that remind him of his latest visits away from home—trips to the beach, gatherings with his friends, and other occasions. Or your child can draw or cut out pictures of favorite toys, foods, clothes, animals, and other objects of special interest. Don't worry about exactness or artistic design. A product he can call his own, which is a reflection of himself, is the important thing.

Activity 193   "Family Tree"

Understanding the Idea of Family
(to help your child appreciate the idea of family
and her place in it)

MATERIALS: A large piece of paper; pen, pencil, or crayon; some old magazines to cut up (optional); your child's drawings of family members, or cutouts representing them.

DIRECTIONS: Use a large piece of paper for the family tree. Draw a square for each family member, and arrange them as in the illustration. Help your child paste a picture or draw a picture representing the person on each square. (For a very young child you might include only the members of her immediate household.) Your child may want to color her box a special color. She might be

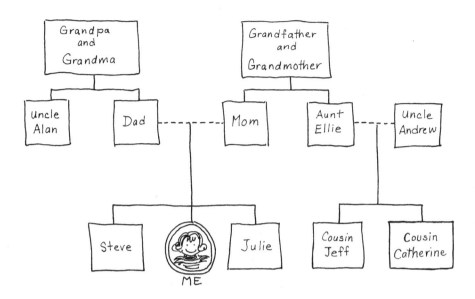

interested to see that horizontal connecting lines are for brothers and sisters, vertical lines are for parents and children, and dotted lines are for husband and wife. If your child is an adoptive or foster child, draw the diagram to include whatever additional relationships, if any, are important to her.*

RELATIONSHIPS WITH OTHERS

Closely allied to self-image is relationships with others. As the previous section stated, it is impossible to separate a child's self-concept from the feedback he receives from others. His relationships with others are important because satisfying interaction with others helps develop a strong and healthy self-esteem.

No one is completely isolated from those around him. Without other people, one would have no sense of self. Individuals who have suffered from severe social isolation resemble persons who

are mentally retarded. The human personality cannot bloom without the stimulation and reflection from others.

In this section there are activities that will heighten your child's awareness of relationships within the family and within her immediate social group. The emphasis is on how we treat others as friends, neighbors, and relatives. A child's behavior toward others inevitably will be reflected back to her. It is vital for your child to experience the joys of social give-and-take as others respond warmly. These activities are intended to help a child gain self-confidence in an enjoyable, positive way.

Activities include suggestions for your child's responses to particular social situations (Activities 194 and 196), changes in routine (Activity 197), ways a child can help within the family (Activity 199), relationships to people outside the home (Activities 195, 198, 200, and 201), conflict resolution (Activities 202 and 203), and cultural diversity (Activities 204 and 205).

Activity 194   *"You're Welcome"*

Using Appropriate Words in Their Proper Social Context
(to help your child learn appropriate social exchanges)

DIRECTIONS: Pass a favorite toy back and forth using the words "Please," "Thank you," or "You're welcome," as appropriate. It will give your child a lot of pleasure to use these words in the right place and observe the warm response she gets from others. You can also practice using other friendly words and phrases with your child such as "Hello," "Goodbye," "I'm sorry," "Excuse me," "See you later," and "Have a nice trip."

Activity 195   *"Happy Birthday"*

Celebrating Birthdays
(to recognize your child's uniqueness and importance
on a special day)

DIRECTIONS: Birthdays have special significance to everyone. It is a day marked especially for each one of us. Help your child plan his own birthday party. Avoid surprise parties. Planning the party with you is as much fun for your child as the party itself. Simple homemade decorations and simple food you and your child can make together are best. Keep the party relatively brief (a few hours). Specify on the invitation when the party is to begin and end. A nice touch for your child's friends, which will also help you know who will be coming, is to include a stamped post card (addressed to your child) along with the invitation. Have his friends check either "I can come" or "I can't come." You can also leave a space for friends to sign their names.*

Activity 196   *"I Can Make You Smile"*

Relating to Others
(to challenge your child's imagination in different social settings)

DIRECTIONS: Ask your child to think of how many ways she can do the following:

*From *Learning Through Play* by Jean Marzollo and Janice Lloyd. Copyright © 1972 by Janice Lloyd and Jean Marzollo. Reprinted by permission of Harper & Row, Publishers, Inc., and William Morris Agency, Inc., on behalf of the authors.

1. Make her friend smile.
2. Show that she likes someone else.
3. Make the dog or cat happy.
4. Do something nice for mother or father.
5. Help around the house.
6. Entertain baby brother or sister (if she has one).

Activity 197   "What's New"

Changes in the Routine
(to help your child adjust to new situations)

DIRECTIONS: Talk with your child about the kinds of changes that can often occur with the people around him. Samples could include:

1. Changes in the family—births, deaths, divorces, marriages, moving.
2. Changes in the neighborhood—new neighbors or houses, new stores, new roads.
3. Changes that occur outside the home—new students at his school, a new teacher, trips he has taken, beginning swimming or piano lessons.

Activity 198   "Tinker, Tailor"

Talking about the Service People Who
Come to Your Home
(to help your child become acquainted with people
and occupations outside the home)

DIRECTIONS: When someone comes to your house to perform a service (plumber, carpenter, washer repairman), discuss with your child what they do and why they do it. Discuss how they help the family. You might want to point out to your child that when *he* needs fixing up, he goes to the office of the doctor or dentist. When your washer, stove, or refrigerator needs fixing, the "appliance doctor" comes to *them*.

Activity 199   "To Market, to Market"

Junior Shopping List for the Supermarket
(to help your child feel her own value as she takes part
in the real work of the family)

DIRECTIONS: Help your child cut out food pictures from the newspaper or magazines. Each of you can make out your own shopping list. You can help her select nutritious foods she likes. Cut out the pictures and paste them on a blank paper, or let your child draw pictures and color them if she wants to. Take the picture list to the store and locate all the items as she shops with you. Let your child take things off the shelf and unload the shopping cart at the checkout counter. For more excitement, you might let her push the cart and pick out the items. You might even let her give the money for some of the items to the checkout person and receive the change. You can have your child help put away the food items you have bought when you get home.

Activity 200   "What Shall I Do for You?"

Caring About People
(to show your child how you can express concern for others)

DIRECTIONS: Discuss with your child how there are many times when other people especially appreciate hearing from us. Someone who is sick is the most obvious example, but you can also talk about how people like to be congratulated for an accomplishment (your child should understand that feeling!). With your child, visit a neighbor or relative who is sick, or talk over with your child how you can make someone feel better. Consider making a card, writing a letter, sending a small gift. Ask your child what things would make him feel better if he were sick in bed or sad about something. Communicating with someone can simply be a nice gesture to brighten his or her day. Your older relatives will love to receive original drawings or scribblings from your child.

Activity 201   "Next Door"

Appreciating Neighbors
(to understand the importance of neighbors to each other)

DIRECTIONS: Talk over with your child who the neighbors are. You can indicate to her that the word "neighbor" comes from an old word "nigh" meaning "near." Visit a neighbor and talk with him or her and your child about how valuable it is to have neighbors. Go over the ways you can be good neighbors—enjoying talking and visiting with each other, helping when someone is sick, borrowing and lending things, giving rides to each other if cars break down, baby-sitting, feeding pets when people are away.

Activity 202   "We Can Work It Out"

Resolving Disagreements
(to model conflict resolution—problem-solving techniques)

DIRECTIONS: If you and your child need to solve a problem or resolve a conflict, you can take the following steps:

1. Explore with him what the problem or conflict seems to be. Try to listen accurately to what he is saying—as calmly, objectively, and nonjudgmentally as possible.

2. Brainstorm (go over) possible solutions with him. All should be listed, even those that seem crazy or impossible. Offer some solutions of your own.

3. Go over the solutions and choose one that is acceptable to both of you. Arriving at consensus (a joint agreement) is an important part of the process.

4. Determine how the solution will be carried out. Discuss the details (who, what, where, when, why) as you find a way to carry it out.

5. Check back after a period of time to see how the solution is working. Make adjustments as necessary at that time.

Activity 203   "She Hit Me"

Examining Family/Neighborhood Conflicts
(to explore the nature of children's conflicts and their resolution)

MATERIALS: Puppets or dolls, magazines, newspapers, crayons or magic markers, drawing and/or writing paper.

DIRECTIONS: Discuss with your child conflicts that have either been in the family or among her friends. They could also be some she has witnessed on the playground, in a store, or elsewhere. For further illustrations, you could produce pictures of

conflicts from magazines or newspapers. You can also use puppets or dolls to help re-create the conflict.

1. Discuss who is at conflict and what the conflict is about. Relate the conflict to your child's own life, if possible.
2. Work out with your child a positive resolution of the conflict either through discussion, drawings, or writing something down.

Activity 204   *"My Family and the World Family"*
Showing the Cultural Diversity of People

MATERIALS: Magazines, newspapers, scissors, paste.

DIRECTIONS: With your child look at various pictures of immediate or more distant members of the family. Describe how they
are related to your child. You can also explain that not all families
have a mother and a father—for example, single-parent families—
and there are not always children. You might also review some of
the many definitions of a family unit such as blended, foster,
adopted, extended, single-sex, children being raised by grandparents or other relatives, intentional communities.

For further information on family diversity, see *Families: A
Celebration of Diversity, Commitment, and Love* by Aylette Jenness
(Boston: Houghton-Mifflin Co., 1990). Also, for children's books
on multiculturalism, see *Our Family, Our Friends, Our World: An An-
notated Guide to Significant Multicultural Books for Children and
Teenagers* by Lyn Miller-Lachmann (New York: R. R. Bowker, 1992).

VARIATION: Extend the concept of family to the idea of the
human family. Assemble magazines and newspapers, and help the
child cut out multicultural examples of members of the human
family. Discuss the similarities and differences between people of
various cultures. You can make a collage, or you can pin some of
the people you cut out on a bulletin board.

Activity 205   *"Different People—Different Traditions"*
Celebrating the Differences and Similarities of Cultural Traditions

DIRECTIONS: Discuss with your child the traditions you have
in your family, then go over some of the traditions found in other
families such as your child's friends. Explain how everyone has

special traditions depending on who they are, where they live, what they celebrate, and what they believe. For example, explore with your child the different ways various cultures celebrate holidays like Christmas or Hanukkah.

ASSUMING RESPONSIBILITY

Assuming responsibility does not have to be associated with tedious chores; such a negative approach causes children to resist. If responsibility springs from positive social relationships within the family, children will usually be cheerful and willing to help around the house, especially if they perceive their tasks as important.

We all need to feel useful, children as well as adults. In addition, a child's emerging sense of competency, which comes with doing things, is important to self-esteem. A young child will take pride in being able to help you with household tasks or in accomplishing jobs on his own. You will never find a young child so willing to wash dishes again as he is in the preschool years! Of course, he needs help and supervision, and you will need to allow an extra fifteen minutes or half hour when you let him help you.

The kitchen floor may be wet and the dishes soapy, but he will be delighted.

Young children often have trouble with the routineness of ordinary jobs or responsibilities. Expect to have to remind children of jobs they do on a regular basis. Try to do this in a friendly, objective way. Avoid creating a feeling of fear and guilt; it dampens the willingness to continue responsible behavior. Similarly, nagging on the parent's part often creates feelings of mutual frustration for parent and child. A child's jobs should remain flexible so that a conflict between parent and child does not result. It is helpful to talk over with your child as much as possible what *she* would like to do, rather than constantly imposing tasks on her. Once she has mastered a task, a child may enjoy jobs more if she is able to switch to a harder, more challenging job. A child also needs a parent to know when to back off or step in and help with the given task. Sharing the task often gives parent and child time to discuss how good it feels to help.

Ideally, responsibility should spring from a child's ability to make judgments and be responsible for his own choices, no matter how small they may be. If your child feels you are interested in what he is thinking and feeling, he is more likely to cooperate with you. Being a good listener and keeping positive and productive lines of communication open are two very good ways of helping your child develop his own sense of responsibility both to himself and to others.

The activities in this section include giving your child an increasing sense of responsibility (Activities 207 and 209), caring for and using books in the library (Activity 210), learning to put away toys and take care of them (Activities 206 and 208), and learning how to deal responsibly and effectively with the environment outside of the home (Activities 211 and 212).

Activity 206   "Clean as a Whistle"

Putting Away Toys
(to help establish responsible behavior with possessions)

DIRECTIONS: When it is time to clean up, set a timer or watch a clock and see if your child can "beat the clock" and still put away the toys in an orderly fashion. Stick to the rules you have set about cleaning up and putting away toys after your child has finished playing with them.

Activity 207   "Making a Picture Chart"

Establishing a Routine
(to create a sense of order in your child's daily routines)

DIRECTIONS: Responsible behavior comes more easily if your child has a routine time for most activities. Make a picture chart of your child's daily routines and try to set a regular time for meals, playing, nap time, bath, errands, and limited television watching. Establishing a regular schedule helps your child create her own internal controls. You can promote self-direction by announcing when certain events are about to happen. For example, you can say, "In five minutes it will be time to eat lunch" or "When that program is over, it's time for your bath." Use a timer, sand glass, alarm clock, or just the clock. It is apt to be easier for a child to accept a nudge from an inanimate gadget than a parent.

Activity 208   "Save My Toys"

Taking Care of Toys
(to develop responsible behavior and attitudes
toward possessions)

DIRECTIONS: Find boxes to store toys of various sizes. Work with your child on a simple organizational scheme for storing toys. When a toy is broken or lost, talk with your child about how he could have prevented this from happening. Try to avoid an accusing or blaming attitude. You and your child might want to invent rules that will prevent toys from being broken in the future.

VARIATION: Discuss ways adults as well as children must take care of certain possessions—for example, washing the car, painting the house, oiling the lawnmower, polishing shoes.

Activity 209   "I Can Do It Myself"

Becoming Independent
(to help your child learn to assume responsibility
and make choices)

DIRECTIONS:

A. *Encourage Work Experiences.* Start off by doing a job the two of you can share. For example:

1. Help her make her bed until she can do it herself.
2. Let her help make the breakfast cereal.
3. Ask him to wipe the table and the counters in the kitchen.
4. Let him take part in making sandwiches.
5. Show her how to help you in the garden with planting, weeding, and watering.
6. Clean up the house together.

B.   *Allow Your Child to Make Choices.* For example, let her choose:

1. Which kind of soup to have for lunch.
2. Which clothes to wear (within reason!).
3. Which color toothbrush to buy.
4. Which kind of cereal to eat.
5. Which household chores she should do.

You should feel overjoyed when you hear your child say, "I want to do it myself!" Try to support your child's early efforts to be independent whenever possible. If she dresses herself, it might take twice as long, but her sense of accomplishment will encourage her to make further efforts.

Activity 210   *"My Books, Your Books"*

Using the Library
(to teach the proper use of books)

DIRECTIONS: Make a trip to the local library with your child. Show him how to find books and how to use them. Let him get his own library card, and help him select books. Encourage him to take responsibility for the care of his library books. Mark the date on the calendar when the books are due, and emphasize how he must get them back on time so he can take out some new ones and how someone else can borrow the ones he will return.

Activity 211   *"Use It Once, Use It Twice"*

Ecology
(to demonstrate responsible behavior toward the environment)

DIRECTIONS: Talk with your child about how we can avoid pollution and waste.*

1. If you have a garden, you can demonstrate a conservation program of your own by using a readily available natural resource: your garbage. Collect all the organic material (eggshells, scraps of food, leaves) and start a compost pile. It's an excellent project to share with your child and it will produce a rich, fertile soil for your garden. *Note:* For further information on how to make compost piles, see *Better Homes and Gardens, Step by Step Landscaping* (Des Moines, IA: Meredith Corp., 1991, p. 235); Reader's Digest, *Illustrated Guide to Gardening* (Pleasantville, NY: The Reader's Digest Associates, Inc., 1993, p. 595); Roger B. Swain, *The Practical Gardener* (New York: Henry Holt and Co., 1991, pp. 147–150).

2. Collect your bottles, aluminum cans, and newspapers, and take a trip with your child to deposit them at a recycling center near you.

3. Conserve paper products as much as possible (for example, use only half a paper towel at a time), and explain to your child the desirability of white paper products, which do not pollute the water supply the way colored ones do.

4. It might interest your child if you show her how we can all take care to save gas, water, and electricity.

Activity 212   *"The World Out There"*

Becoming Involved in the Community
(to expand your child's immediate social experiences)

DIRECTIONS: Even though their social experiences are necessarily limited, young children gain in social maturity and control by participating in activities like the following:

1. Story hour at the local library.

2. Swimming or dancing lessons at a local club or "Y."

---

*From *Learning Through Play* by Jean Marzollo and Janice Lloyd. Copyright © 1972 by Janice Lloyd and Jean Marzollo. Reprinted by permission of Harper & Row, Publishers, Inc., and William Morris Agency, Inc., on behalf of the authors.

3. Sunday school.

4. Various kinds of summer recreation programs.

5. A nursery school or day care center.

INDEX